Erica Van Horn

Living Locally

Uniformbooks 2014

First published 2014, reprinted 2019
with assistance from

A Purse for Books

Copyright © Erica Van Horn
ISBN 978-1-910010-02-0

Uniformbooks
7 Hillhead Terrace, Axminster, Devon EX13 5JL
www.uniformbooks.co.uk

Trade distribution in the UK by Central Books
www.centralbooks.com

Printed and bound by T J International, Padstow, Cornwall

Foreword

Long ago I spent one of the happiest years of my life living in what was then countryside around Dublin. I remember being struck by the way friends and family there enjoyed using the word "desperate" as if it contained soft humour against the rush of silence. In *Living Locally* Erica Van Horn has produced a meticulous field guide of what it means to be an American discovering the embedded, entangled mysteries of being Irish. Van Horn finds these ambivalences everywhere: "Hill farmers used to take their sheepdogs down to the sea every year to soothe or maybe to toughen their feet in the salt water." In Ireland stones and dreams are things one contends with, navigates daily. "A blow-in is anyone who moves here from somewhere else." It is too much to say that Ireland's landscape necessarily produces a poet or an artist; yet, if you are going to be in Ireland it helps to be one.

Van Horn and Simon Cutts have been living on what was once a small farm not far from Clonmel in the hills of South Tipperary Ireland, since 1996. There they write, make art, and make books. She celebrates (often with barbed asides) the myriad loops and perimeters of the particular decisions forming family and village life. From exploratory walks with her dog to talking in the pub, Van Horn observes this world, by always circulating within it.

The small details that constitute place accrue: There is a murder in Mary Corbett's house just down the road. Cellophane cones are tied to the hedges around the murder cottage. A Peruvian llama is living in a field nearby, in another stands a gloomy donkey. In March, on a bright morning the ground under the apple tree is covered with wild garlic. Shallykabukies are little snails with yellowy striped shells.

These specifics become insistent. "The intermittent rain is annoying. The sunny moments are beautiful, hot and drying, but the rain is winning and we are all sick of it." Yet, in that persistence the particularities all add up to what we call, on lucky days, the full test of life. "Desperate is the word. The Irish do not have 300 words for rain. They have 'desperate' and 'soft'." Day after day, winter and summer, almost always veiled with rain which rules all activities but makes the flowers brighter and gives one time to write. In Van Horn's words, one recollects the ordinary all over again.

What I saw was as small and poor as it was large and significant, as modest as it was charming, as near as it was good, and as delightful as it was warm.

—Robert Walser

27 June 2007—Tom Browne told me about the dances held in the village halls when he was young. He said the girls were always on the look-out for the men with wrinkles in the back of their jackets. The wrinkles meant that a man had arrived by motor car. Those men who arrived without wrinkles had traveled on foot or by bicycle, and so they were considered second best.

2 July—The rain is driving us all mad. We have had wild and blustery, partly dry weather for the last two days, but rain is still the main topic of conversation. Rain rules all our activities. If I am down in the barn doing something and torrential rains start, I look around for something else to do until the rain stops. Sometimes an hour or so passes and lots of jobs get done before escape is possible. All this makes for a kind of erratic approach to any activity, because constant interruption creates a constant need for re-directed energy. If we didn't have our work spread out between four buildings it might be easier. If our work wasn't always and mostly about paper, it might be easier too. Wet paper is a problem. Clothes and skin and hair dry eventually, but wet paper is a pest.

3 July—We still have not had a complete day without rain. We still have not identified the blue flower on the grass roof. We still have not finished folding and collating our book pages. But we have completed our bathroom. We now have a sink for the first time in nine years. We have become so accustomed to using the bathtub for brushing our teeth that it is a shock not to continue doing so. John Carney designed a towel rail which is also a radiator. He built it out of welded copper pipes, and hooked it up to the radiator entrance and exit pipes. It looks like a huge and rather wide ladder. In the winter, we shall have warm places to hang the towels, but for now, it is good just to have any place at all to hang towels. A little more painting, and carpentry, and we can stop this bath-room work.

6 July—Liam Harper telephoned. He is the meter reader for the Electricity Board. He rings every so often, probably four times a year, to ask for a reading off our electricity meter. I have to fetch a chair to climb up and read the numbers. Sometimes I have to get a torch

too. He always tells me to be careful not to fall off the chair. I do not think he has ever come here in person, even at the beginning. I have no idea what he looks like but I imagine a very large man sitting in an armchair in front of the television with a cigarette, a big mug of tea, and a jumble of papers. On the telephone, Liam Harper sounds like a large and jolly man. He is probably slim and sitting at an organized desk, not smoking.

16 July—We keep hearing things on the radio and reading in the English papers about the way the English are dealing with their new smoking ban. I do not remember hearing very much about the Scottish situation in dealing with it. We have so thoroughly accepted and grown accustomed to the smoking ban here in Ireland, it is just normal. I cannot even recall how many years it has been since it began. The really big discussions all took place before the ban went into effect. Once it was law, everyone found a way to deal with it and the non-smokers kind of forgot that it was an issue, except when someone came down from the mountains

or something and really had not had to acknowledge it yet.

One Michael came into the pub shortly after the law took effect. He ordered a pint and slapped his pack of cigarettes onto the counter. Rose took them away and said he could have them when he left. He cursed roundly, and then went out to his car to get a cigar, which he had 'in storage'. Rose bolted the door after him. After smoking the cigar halfway, he wailed and shouted that he was perished out there, and that she had to let him back in since it was no way to treat a 75-year-old respected customer. Later that night, another Michael came in, had two pints, and then went outside and smoked ten cigarettes, one right after another.

23 July—Another call from the Station Master at Waterford Railway Station. We have not spoken for some weeks now. He said, "Hello, Erica, I understand you've been ringing me again." I said, "Oh really? Did I? And what did I say?" We both laughed and he expressed his regret that it had not been him who had answered the phone this time. Some months ago, a woman rang to complain about the road being closed at the level crossing for an excessively

long time, just in the morning when she was driving to work. Of course, that was exactly when the train needed to go by too. The Station Master assured her that the road was never closed for a minute longer than was necessary. The second time, she left her name and number. When he rang back, he got me. He knew immediately that he had a different woman on the line. My voice was a dead giveaway. I was obviously not the woman with the strong Tipperary accent. I did not even know which level crossing was being discussed. The same woman phones and complains on a regular basis, and she always claims to be me. The Station Master marvels that she does not try to find an alternative route for driving to work. He always rings to tell me when I have phoned.

5 August—We had ten solid hours of heavy, heavy rain last night. It never let up. The morning has been soft and drizzly. I walked out with Em. She's a dog, so wet is okay. Her mother was a sheepdog. We don't know who her father was. He might have been a bearded collie. She has the black and white coloration of a sheepdog but she has shorter legs, wider hips, and a large fluffy white ruff around her neck. She is not all sheepdog.

As we walked, I was surprised to find blackberries ready to pick. It does not seem possible that there has been enough sun for them to have had time to ripen. They are several weeks, maybe even a month, early. The hedgerows are full of wild honeysuckle with the blackberries tucked in between. Here in Tipperary, hedges are called ditches. I cannot get myself used to calling them ditches. Ditches divide one field from another field or from a road. A ditch is high growth, and what I would call a ditch is called a dike here. So I should rephrase this: The ditches are full of wild honeysuckle with the blackberries tucked in between. The smell of it all is amazingly sweet. And still, deep mud squelches underfoot.

20 August—I was in the barn, with the door open and Em lying just inside, when a fox went racing past. He was only inches from the door. I was out and running before I was even certain what I had seen. Em was way ahead of me, barking like mad down through the meadow. I just managed to see the fox disappear into the trees. I have no idea why I ran after it. Em was never going to catch a fox and I have no desire to catch one, nor for her to catch one. We often see the fox going through the field, but never so near to us or the buildings. We always speak of The Fox. And The Fox is always He. This spring we saw a baby fox in the boreen. It was as startled as

we were. It had a large head on its very small body. Its presence suggests a fox father and a fox mother, and now a fox family. I guess it was that baby, now an adolescent, who ran by the barn and got us all excited.

11 September—Yesterday there was a big party for Paddy in the pub. Well, it was not actually for Paddy because he died last summer, but it was a party in his spirit. There were raffles and prizes to raise money for a headstone for his grave, or for a plaque to celebrate his music or both. As soon as the party idea was mooted, the hunt was on for the bikinis. Seven years ago, for Paddy's 70th birthday, Simon and I decided to make decorations. We spent an entire day making dozens of Yellow Polka-Dot Bikinis out of paper, paint and ribbons. The party back then was a surprise for Paddy, so we had to sneak into the bar in the afternoon and hang what looked like washing lines and the many bikini bottoms and tops with clothes pegs all around the place.

It was amazing to see the bar so festive and bright. The favourite song was sung again and again that night.

I always assumed that the bikinis just got ripped down and thrown away after the party. I did spot a few that Christmas, tucked into various wreathes and decorations around the village. We were surprised to hear last week that Rose had rescued several lines of them after the party. She spent a few days trying to find them in her house.

Yesterday we were there again, at 5 o'clock, draping the last two lines of bikinis, and carefully pushing the cups back into bra-like shape after them having been squished in a bag for so long. We made a large photo blow-up of Paddy singing with his hand cupped and his nails tapping on the table as he always did. The party went on and on, with singing and laughter until 2am when Rose threw everyone out. I later heard that about 20 people were still outside singing at 4am.

3 October—I pick blackberries daily. They seem to be going on and on this year. There is a lot of variation from bush to bush. Someone told me there can be thirteen varieties growing all in near proximity to one another. Or was it thirty? Once they are all mixed up in my bag or my bowl, they are just blackberries.

Around here, people are suspicious of blackberries. They are convinced that the berries are full of maggots and that the maggots will make them sick. It is nearly impossible to convince anyone otherwise, and as a result I never see anyone picking blackberries. One bit of advice I was given is to soak the berries in hot water with plenty of salt in it before eating them. This is a terrible thing to do to blackberries. No wonder no one wants to eat blackberries, and no wonder no one likes them.

17 October—As we drove home from the airport, we heard news on the radio of a murder in Grange. As we got closer, we realized it had happened in the little house just to the right below our boreen. It was at Mary Corbett's old house. Once we got near, we were stopped by the Gardai who had closed off the road for forensic testing. People in white suits and special booties were everywhere. We could see our road just up ahead, but we had to turn and take a long and circuitous route home. It is difficult to believe this. Already London is miles away.

20 October—More news of the murder. Everyone speaks in hushed voices about nothing else. The young girl (20) was killed by her boyfriend (30), who then stabbed her brother (23) and ran to the neighbour's house to wash his hands. No one really knows exactly what happened. This is roughly how it is reported. There is a lot of speculation and a lot of theory. The brother is in Intensive Care in Cork.

9 November—The Murder Cottage looks bleak. There are cellophane cones still tied to the hedge outside. The messages on cards are visible, but the flowers, which were inside the cellophane, have died. Teddy bears are lined up in one of the windows. Just seeing them reminds us of how very young the dead girl was. The car and motorcycle remain in the yard. Everything there seems to be in a sort of limbo.

12 November—The car has been removed from the little house. The motorcycle is still there but it seems to be in pieces. I spoke with a neighbour and heard a lot of quite horrific details, most of which I wish I had not heard. Apparently 40,000 euro was found in the

house, which supports the theories of drug-dealing. The Garda Drug Squad was down from Dublin during the three days while the road was closed off.

16 November—The little house has been cleared, both inside and out. The cellophane flower wrappers are gone, as is the motorcycle, the washing on the line, the teddy bears, and the blue towel. We understand the house is up for rent.

23 November—I am interested in the naming of bread here. White bread is always spoken of as A Pan of Bread. If it is sliced, it is A Sliced Pan of Bread. It might be shortened to just A Pan, or even Half a Pan. Sometimes it is A Sliced Pan. It is not as if one is buying this bread tipped directly out of a pan. It might be a loaf (Pan) sitting on the bakery shelf, or it might be A Sliced Pan wrapped in waxed paper. Brown soda bread is called Brown Bread. The mixture is shaped and put onto a baking tray before cooking. So I guess because it is not made in a pan, and the white yeast bread is, the word Pan is what defines the difference. A Pan is a Unit of Bread.

10 December—The last few days have been wild and windy with buckets of rain. The inside of the car flooded just because the rain was driven at it in such an unlikely direction. The river is flooded and fields on both sides of the road are under water. These blustery days are on top of a week of much rain. The ground cannot absorb any more. A man fell into the river in Cahir on Saturday night and has not been found yet. There are rescue people stationed on all the bridges with binoculars, looking and looking up and down the river trying to spot the body. Last night we were told that the only way to locate the body at this stage is to put a bale of hay out into the river with a lit candle stuck into the top of it. The bale will float and float until it is exactly over the body and then it will stop and hover until the body is recovered. This is such a mad idea that I cannot even begin to think about it, but there seems to be a consensus of opinion that this is indeed a tried and true method.

11 December—Sign seen on the road to Youghal:

RISK OF
FALLEN
OR FALLING
ROCKS

16 December—A Blow-in is anyone who moves here from some-where else. It is not exactly negative but there is the implication that this person will not stay and will most likely blow out again. A Blow-in can be someone from 3,000 miles away or it can be some-one from the next village.

28 December—Outside the shop, an older woman stopped to ask me about Emily, and then continued on, by herself, about dogs in general. I gathered that her ramble came from the fact that she still is not used to the idea that dogs are being given people names. She felt more comfortable with a time when all dogs were called names like Rover, Whitey, Blackie, Sandy, Partner or Pal. Dogs were spoken of by two names: their own and the name of their owner. If there were three dogs named Whitey in one area, they'd be known as Whitey Ryan, Whitey O'Dwyer, and Whitey Sweeney, so you would know which Whitey was being discussed.

I added surnames for some local dogs, just to see how they'd sound. We have Ben O'Keefe, Max Scully, Sam Costigan, Clint Browne, Milo Condon, Susie Hally, Ginger McGrath, Coco Shine, and the late, great Sydney O'Byrne-Casey.

29 December—We drove out to do some errands today and admired several huge Christmas trees installed by the local council at road intersections and in little lay-bys. These trees have been decorated with silver foil-covered plastic drinks bottles. Most of the bottles are the 1.5 or the 2 litre sort. They blow about like mad in this wind. A fair number of old CDs add to the sparkly effect. The most decorated house in the area is in Ardfinnan. It has hundreds of white lights which outline the shape of the house, the bushes and the trees as well as making a multitude of other shapes like stars and things. It is a shock to come down the hill and to catch sight of this mayhem when usually one only sees the river, and then the mountains off in the distance. At night, there is only darkness. These Christmas lights get more elaborate every year. The house was featured on the television. The man who lives in this well-lit house is blind.

9 January 2008—There is a bit in the newspaper about Father Condon, the local priest, who is leaving to take up his new post as Parish Priest in Ballyduff Upper, County Waterford. There was a going-away party for him where "the people of the village presented him with A Wad of Notes on behalf of the Parishioners".

14 January—The Gloomy Donkeys are back. There are four of them and they seem to move from field to field in the neighbourhood and then disappear for a while. They always look miserable. They make a mournful baying sound. I understood that one donkey alone was a bad idea because it would be lonely, but that in pairs they were happy. These four never look happy. They never romp or move quickly or lightly. They show no interest in the dogs or people who stop to look or speak to them. Horses amble over to a fence to see what might happen and cows can get excited and rush around. These four are always gloomy. They were in the meadow beside the murder cottage at the time of the killing. I would like to say that that's what made them so gloomy but I would be lying. They were already like that.

31 January—I am interested in the change of shoes. This used to be a country of dusty shoes. Today more people are wearing trainers. And everyone has more than one pair of shoes. Houses are surrounded by gravel, or concrete, or tarmacadam. Most people never get anywhere near to soil or mud. There is no dust to gather on your shoes unless you are working as a plasterer or doing something with cement. I rarely see lace-up leather shoes with a healthy coating of dust.

23 February—Liam Boyle came down with two other men in a car. They were counting badgers. Or accounting for badgers? Liam lost a few cows to TB so he is always worried about the badger population. This year, we have seen less badger activity than ever. I have not even seen a dead badger.

Liam Boyle is the man from whom we got the slates for one side of our barn roof. He let us take them off a falling down building on his land. He would not accept money, so we made him a cake. Whenever he comes down, he nods at the roof, and says, "Roof's holding up okay." I never know if this is meant as a statement of fact or as a question.

20 March—I think the moon is full tonight. It looks like the moon is full tonight. Em went to take a drink at the little low water butt

from which she likes to drink. She jumped away in surprise because the reflection was so bright.

10 April—Em and I took a different walk today. It is an old walk with both fields and road. We have not taken this route since last summer. It was a nice, quiet and exploratory walk. Everything was familiar and everything, as always, was completely new.

21 April—The primroses are blooming all down the boreen. As we walked along this morning, we noted how many there are and how lovely they are this year. We comment on how many there are and how lovely they are every year.

29 April—A booklet came in the post today. *Preparing for Major Emergencies: An Introduction* comes from the Office of Emergency Planning. It covers Animal Diseases, Fire, Flooding, Nuclear Incidents, Pandemic Influenza, Hazardous Chemical Spills, Explosions and Suspicious Packages, as well as Accidents at Sea. There are tips for planning and first aid, and useful telephone numbers. The fat shiny booklet is printed in both Irish and English. I will put it into the cupboard with our Post-Nuclear Fall-Out Potassium Iodate Tablets, in the hope that we shall never have need for any of them.

30 April—I spoke to Kenneth while out walking with Em. We chatted about this and that. I said I had not seen the Gloomy Donkeys for a while. He said that they get moved from field to field, so every once in a while they end up back in their owner's own fields. He told me that these are not just any old Gloomy Donkeys, but that they are very special French Donkeys which their owner breeds to  sell. He said each donkey sells for 2,000 euro. He told me that the same man also has a llama. I feel depressed by both these pieces of news.

7 May—A dead cow in Joe's farmyard. It has that 'legs up in the air but at an impossible angle' look. It is the look of a cow that was dragged there by man or machine. No cow dies with its legs like

that. Em and I both examined it, she at much closer range than me. I hope it is gone tomorrow.

8 May—We are having some trouble with the broadband again, so after trying various solutions, we called the office. It seems the whole company has been sold and the new owners are now based in Waterford. While trying to find out the name of the new company, we were told that it was bought by the guy who owned it.

10 May—There is a new tenant in Mary Corbett's cottage. (The Murder Cottage. The House That Nobody Will Ever Live In Again. The House That They Will Have To Tear Down.) This new tenant is puttering about outside all the time. He seems to be a real baling twine and duct tape kind of man. His car has a droopy bumper, so he poked two holes in it and laced some string through the holes. The strings are attached to something under the car's bonnet. When the bonnet is closed, the strings are tightened and the bumper no longer drags on the ground. I am interested each time I pass to see what he is doing or what he has done. Em is interested because he has a puppy.

12 May—The cow parsley is in bloom. The grassy sides of the roads are getting that frothy look that only cow parsley can give them. As more and more blossoms appear, it becomes truly

luxurious. The boreen is so narrow that the drive down to the house becomes a natural car wash on a damp day or a dewy morning. As I walk, I like to pick a large piece of cow parsley and wave it about in time with my stride. This morning I was making large horizontal figure eights as I walked at a fast pace down the hill. While I walked and lashed my cow parsley through the air, I sang a whishing kind of chant. Maybe I should not call it singing. It is: FWEE HAH, FWEE HAH, FWEE FWEE FWEE HAH. I seem to be able to chant this endlessly. I can speed it up or slow it down. It's the same tuneless chant that appears in my mouth every year when the cow parsley appears. I was a bit surprised to find myself being watched over the hedge by a local farmer this morning. I did not say hello for fear of having to explain myself.

I just waved my cow parsley at him and kept walking and chanting and lashing.

9 June—I went to the SuperValu in Cahir today. It was very busy so I went to the far end of the car park. I had forgotten about the plaster Madonna who stands at the corner, to the left of the bottle banks. She is just off the tarmac, raised up on a pedestal, where the hedges meet. Maybe I had only forgotten about her because the bushes had grown over her. Someone has just done a careful job of trimming the hedges up to and around her. She now has her own little green aura.

10 June—I forgot to mention the other thing I saw in Cahir yesterday. The Warehouse of Wonderful Art has re-opened. It is only a summer thing, probably because the windows are missing throughout the building. I think the building was once a grain store. It sits on the opposite end of the bridge from Cahir Castle. At Christmas, there are usually Christmas trees sold from there. Each window has a plank of wood covering about a third of its opening. There is no glass. For the summer, a painting is displayed on each plank, in each window, four stories high. I think that is about 16 or 20 windows which means one can view at least 16 or 20 paintings from the road while driving past, or from the pavement across the road if one is walking.

17 June—There are a lot of new-born calves around. I must find out why they are separated from their mothers. One Joe has a red tank which can be pulled behind his tractor. The tank has bright pink rubber teats all around it, at just the right height for the calves. The other Joe has a blue plastic container which hangs from the side of a gate. This is also at the right height for calves. He has a smaller number of calves and they jostle to drink from the single row of teats. In their excitement, a lot of milk gets spilled on the ground. Em sneaks her head under the gate to lick up the spilt milk. When she does this the young ones back up and stare. I don't know if the staring is disbelief or just interest.

18 June—Tom Smoke is dead. He died as a result of being trapped in a burning apartment. He was from the Nire Valley and owned a house and some land out there. Some of the fields got sold off when he went to live inside in the town. At first it was because he followed a woman there, but then he stayed for the company and for the variety the town offered.

After the funeral, there was a whole evening down at The Hidden Inn with people telling one Tom Smoke story after another. Tom Smoke had great long sideburns which flared out at the bottom, and long thin hair. It was a look like no one else in this decade, and he had a way of living in this time as if it was another time too.

Tom Smoke lost his driving license at one point, and spent some weeks in Limerick Jail. He came out raving about how great the food was and how wonderful that it was served right to you three times a day.

Tom Smoke called every woman Mary. It was alright if your name really was Mary, but, if not, you had no choice. One whose name really is Mary is known as Mary the Half-Way, because she runs a bar called The Half-Way House. It is sort of equidistant between Clonmel and Dungarvan. Tom Smoke went in there one day all bloody. Mary the Half-Way asked him what had happened. He said he had fallen down. She said "Ah well, Our Lord had three falls before he died. There's no shame in it." Tom Smoke answered, "Yeah, but Our Lord didn't fall off a Honda 50."

Tom Smoke got his name years ago from cadging cigarettes. He did not want to buy a whole pack in order to keep himself from smoking in the morning. He would get a smoke off someone in the bar and then buy them a drink in payment. It was an expensive way to be a smoker. No one ever spoke of him simply as Tom. He was always Tom Smoke.

21 June—I found out why the calves are separated from their mothers. I thought it was to make them strong, brave and independent. The real reason is that both of these Joes run dairy farms. They last thing they want is for the mother's milk to go down the throat of a calf. Instead, the babies are fed a formula so they can grow strong quickly and start eating grass. Their fattening formula is exactly what Em does not need.

24 July—We were down in the pub at the end of the afternoon. The whole family of the murdered girl was there. We had heard that the trial had ended that day and that the murderer had been sentenced to life for the murder of the girl and to 15 additional years for the stabbing of her brother. The trial had begun only a few days before and the murderer had begun by pleading Not Guilty. The police had about a hundred witnesses lined up for various degrees of observations, witnessing and character assessments. One neighbour told us that she was number 79, and did not know when

or if she might be called to go down to Cork. The very next day, the murderer changed his plea to Guilty for the murder. Today, he pleaded Guilty to the stabbing assault and the case ended immediately with his sentencing.

The entire family had been in the court, but then they were all in the bar together waiting for the 6 o'clock news as if it would be news to them. There was a lot of rushing in and out of the toilets and from the outside smoking areas, and finally everyone was gathered along the bar (several people deep). The news of the trial and the sentencing came on. The whole bar went silent. There was no cheering, nor cursing. I was worried that everyone would go wild. I was wishing we were not there. Instead, the whole family just moved outside as a group, and they all lit cigarettes. The father joined them a few minutes later. He had missed the whole thing because he was in the toilet.

29 July—We have had a small brown wren inside for most of the day. We chased her around, trying to catch her gently. Wherever she was, she would swoop and rush and suddenly be on the other side of the room. We closed doors to keep her contained but she was able to whiz through the smallest cracks. Each time we thought she was gone, she would reappear rushing out of a cupboard, or down from a high shelf. Finally we gave up. Every window and door was opened and ready for her departure, but she did not want to leave. Simon named her Nuala Quirke, which is his latest favourite Irish name. Now when we say Nuala Quirke, Em rushes out the door barking with excitement.

30 July—Two nights and a lot of daylight hours of solid lashing rain. The ground is sodden and the puddles are enormous. Breda and I managed a rapid walk around through fields and onto the road without even needing rain jackets this morning. We met Pa and Peggy at the entrance to one of their fields. Immediately the conversation turned to a discussion of the rain and to the huge number of shallykabukies seen. They all exclaimed and commented as to how they were seeing vast numbers of shallykabukies and in places where they had never before seen a shallykabuky. I had no idea what they were talking about. I had to interrupt to ask.

Shallykabukies are the little snails with yellowy striped shells, which I had noticed were quite plentiful after rain, but I never knew they had a special name. It must be a word from the Irish, so I will have to find out. No doubt my phonetic spelling leaves a bit to be desired. Even misspelled, it is a grand word.

6 August—I drove to Kilkenny in the rain and got there just in time to catch the train to Dublin. The small station was full of people waiting to board. No one wanted to wait outside in the rain. When the train pulled in, the cars were lettered A, B, E, D, E. My ticket said C, so I decided the first E was probably doubling as a C. I got in and asked a woman if this was C. She said it didn't matter, and

that I should just sit down. I looked for my seat which was Number C32. There was an elderly man sitting in my seat, so I moved along to another one. A second woman told me that the seat numbers don't matter, and that we could just sit anywhere. The conductor came along to punch our tickets. I asked him if it was okay for me to take a later train back. I was booked for the 15.05 return. He said, "Fine." I said, "It's okay then?" He said: "If you have a ticket you can get on any train. It doesn't matter."

The whole train smelled like bacon. Everyone was talking at top speed and top volume. It was impossible to read or to sleep. Nothing matters.

7 August—Simon went down to the pub tonight. He had a chat about wind turbines with the brother of the murdered girl. We never remember this brother's name. We all remember the name of the brother who was stabbed nine times, and whom no one thought would live. Now that brother is back and alive and treated with great respect and kindness. Everyone is gentle. They ask him how he is doing, and they try not to stare at the huge knife wound around his neck.

8 August—There is a new priest in the village. He was in the bar tonight, talking to everyone and admiring Des Dillon's picture of Paddy on the wall. Brendan did a very fine imitation of Paddy singing 'Do What You Do Do Well' for him. Rose got out an album and started to show photographs to illustrate the local history.

I would not have known the man was a priest. He was wearing a green and white striped rugby shirt and jeans and drinking pints of lager. I thought he was someone's relative who was in a great mood because he was visiting from Dublin or somewhere.

18 August—A dead mouse in the wine cupboard. A good chunk of hair and flesh was stuck to the bottle I pulled out. It is not a fresh corpse. There is no smell at all. Still, I wonder what sort of job I can promise in exchange for Simon cleaning it up.

23 September—We just learned that Will Cotter is dead. He hanged himself in his house on Thursday and he was found on Friday. The removal took place on Sunday and he was buried on Monday. It is sad, both the suddenness of it all, and the taking of his own life. He always seemed such a cheerful man. He was from up the Nire. I think there was some family, but he had been living on his own in the village for a few years now.

He came up to get a door from us one day. It was a door that we got when the butcher's shop was being redone. They were throwing out the door and we thought it might fit our shed, but it didn't. When Will Cotter mentioned that he needed a door for his own garden shed, we offered him this door and he happily came to take it away. While he was here, he looked carefully at everything we were growing. He loved gardening. After that visit, he would often leave old books about gardening in the bar for me. When I was finished with them, I would give them back to Rose and eventually he would collect them and then leave me another. He gave me one to keep. It is called Hardy Fruit Growing and it had belonged to his mother. It was often hard to understand Will, because of the drink and because of his lack of teeth. I liked the fact that we communicated with these books about growing things.

Will Cotter loved to dance. He would jump in his car with a friend and head off to a dance in Durrow, which is more than an hour's drive from here. He should never have driven that far. He should never have driven anywhere, since I think he was never not drinking, and he never drank just a little. He liked to dance so much that if there was music, sometimes he danced around the bar with a sweeping brush.

Will Cotter was tall and thin, and very graceful. In the shock of hearing of his death, we were stunned to find out that he was only sixty-five. I just assumed he must be in his late seventies. He wrote a note before he hanged himself. It ended with the words "And God bless you all." The priest read the note out loud at the funeral and ended his own talk by saying, "And God bless you too, Will Cotter."

30 September—There is a Baby Gloomy Donkey in the meadow now. I don't know where the other three adults have gone, but the Baby and Mother stand around together looking as gloomy as ever. How can a baby look so miserable?

6 October—The best thing about Clonmel in the autumn is the smell of apples which fills the whole town. The big cider makers have huge production facilities on the outskirts of town but for some reason there are still these long narrow yards, with high sides, where apples get dumped and maybe weighed right in the middle of town. The access to these dumping places is down a small alley so it cannot be easy for a big truck or a trailer load of apples to be delivered there, much less to be collected and taken away again. My theory is that they keep this town centre delivery place for the apples just to remind everyone that this is cider country. It is a wonderful smell, but such a pity that the cider they produce is so homogenized and un-appley. By the time they are done with it, it could be made of anything. The only good part is the smell of the apples on delivery.

10 October—I went to visit Tom Browne in the residential home. My timing was poor because I interrupted his favourite television programme. He didn't turn it off, but he lowered the volume and let his eyes flick over it every once in a while as we chatted. This programme is about forensic science and it shows police from various departments in the USA. They solve every single crime that comes along, and the solution is always in the attention to tiny, tiny details. Tom often watches this programme. He watches the re-runs of it too, which is why he was not bothered about being interrupted today.

Among other things, we talked about the surprise of Will Cotter's death. Apparently, Tom was not surprised. He said he had known, for as many years as he'd known Will, that he would end his life by his own hand. He was most interested to tell me that he had spent a long time figuring out how Will could have hanged himself in his new, single-storey bungalow. Will Cotter was a tall man, so a door would not have worked. Tom thought and thought and he finally figured out that Will would have opened the little trap door into the attic space and looped a rope over a beam and down into the house. Tom was pleased with himself. He had never visited the scene of the death, but he had managed to solve one aspect of the suicide while sitting in his wheelchair, in between episodes of his favourite programme.

13 October—Suddenly everyone seems to be painting. The hairdresser's premises in the village is now a bright, bright white. It is startling in its whiteness. Kenneth's house is being painted a soft yellow with a lot of white in it, but bright. The little house belonging to the O'Keefes, who own the Late Late Shop, has also been painted white, but this is a quiet white. And almost immediately, surely before the paint has had time to dry, they have new tenants installed.

21 October—The car broke down yesterday. The accelerator cable snapped and the car stopped. A man helped me to get down to the village after instructing me to drive at about two miles an hour. I managed to deliver my elderly friend and her messages to her house, then I deserted the car. John gave me and my two big boxes of books a lift home. He even carried them down to the barn for me. He looked at our new, very square wood pile and asked if that was wood for fuel or just for decoration. Today the tow-truck picked up the car and took it to Mike. I do not like to think how many times I have broken down in that same car.

27 October—The big move around is still going on down at the shop. Now there is a huge empty space in the middle as you walk in. I told Martina that they could have a dance in that space. She said it was all ready for The Siege of Ennis. I had no idea what that could be. She told me that it is a dance done with lots of people at a wedding party, changing partners and making lines. I didn't really understand it but now I hope to be invited to a wedding where it happens.

2 November—It has been a busy day and it is only lunchtime now. Em and I walked up the boreen and Around. That is one of our usual walks. We just call it Around and we know exactly which walk we are speaking about.

We saw Seamus and Teresa outside in their yard. They had a shiny brown puppy with them which had arrived the night before and they did not want to put it back out onto the road. It was a friendly little dog, obviously fed and cared for. They thought it might have run off after being frightened by Halloween fireworks. Both their dogs and Em ignored it. The cats too were uninterested. Seamus kept moaning that he was hopeless about animals and that he would never be able to turn one away. He didn't want another dog but how could he refuse a stray?

Seamus and I put the dog onto a lead with a collar borrowed from their small dog, Sandy, and we walked down the road to ask at a few houses. Mickey the Boxer was seeing to cows in his field. He had no idea whose dog it was, but he told us that it was a pit bull puppy. My feelings for the dog changed immediately. We went farther down the road. Kenneth had been up a ladder painting his house a bit more before going to mass. He had pulled on his work overalls, but now, on taking them off, he found the top of his suit jacket and his tie and shirt and shoes were all speckled with primrose yellow. His trousers were paint free. He did not recognize the dog. After that, Em and I walked home, but Seamus continued along the road to talk to other people. Teresa had phoned around and people were to be outside waiting for Seamus so they could have a viewing of the lost dog.

3 November—Teresa rang last night to say that the puppy had been claimed. Dessie, the man who is renting Mary Corbett's house (The Murder Cottage), came by asking if they had seen the puppy. I knew he had a small dog, and I know what it looked like so I never even considered that this would be his dog. He told Teresa that it was his mother's dog. He told Teresa that he had given it to his mother and then she decided that she didn't want it, so she gave it back to him. We marveled about this over the phone. What kind of son gives his mother a pit bull terrier as a pet?

16 December—We took Em in to the vet for x-rays this morning and picked her up in the afternoon. The vet took us into a room, showed us the x-rays and said that her condition is a cruciate ligament tear. He explained that the cruciate is a ligament that crosses over the dog's equivalent of a knee. We could see the wear on the bones as a result of the ligament

not working correctly any more. There are various options but first we need to get her weight down. I had been doing well with this before we went away, but one month at the kennels and hanging around in Alma's kitchen put loads of weight back on. Fat dogs are more apt to get this ailment, and if it is not solved, the other leg will go too. The surgeon who specializes in this will not even consider operating on a fat dog. So we have three weeks to reduce her volume. With the help of anti-inflammatory drugs and box-rest, we might not need the surgery. Box-rest is a scary thing. The vet said she should be kept in a space no bigger than 1 metre 80 square. He said we should then carry her outside and put her on the grass to do her business. Em is far too lady-like for that. The closest to the house she would go is out behind the barn, never in proximity to the house and never in sight of anyone.

17 December—Simon went to the bank to change some yen into euro. When the woman gave him the rate and the price for the money exchange, he asked if the fee could be waived because he was over sixty. The woman looked up his account details and said he was not registered for Golden Years. He said, "Okay, but look at me. Can't you tell my age by looking at me?" She waived the fee.

18 December—We were off to Kilkenny today so we thought we would take Em in the back of the old station wagon, since that is a restricted space where she could rest quietly. Besides, she enjoys being in towns where she can watch people and activity from the windows. I think of it as her version of going to the cinema.

We don't have one of those metal grid things that keep a dog from moving around the car, so Simon said he would make something. He made a little wooden frame. He said there was absolutely no way she could get through it. We left her in the parked car with a bowl of water, her new car bed and the barricade. One hour later, I returned to drop off some shopping before lunch. Em was sitting in the front seat, behind the steering wheel. She had climbed through Simon's device, without dislodging it, dropped into the back seat and squeezed through to the front. None of this good for the ligament, I'm sure.

We stopped at the timber yard and asked Kevin to make a little picket fence structure so that we can reduce her movements but still have her in the middle of our lives, as usual. We don't really want to do it, but we know we must.

6 January 2009—I went back to the library today to return the books I took out just before Christmas. When I walked in, I was greeted by the same elderly woman with whom I had had a chat that day. She was returning her books too. We had both been looking through the table of recent acquisitions. She told me that she found it terrifying to think of going through the Christmas period without a supply of reading material at hand. She had brought her elderly sister with her that day, so that she could take out four books on her own card and four books on her sister's card. All the books were for herself. Her sister was blind and deaf, and sat quietly nearby during this conversation. I asked if she could have just brought her sister's library card and not her sister since the sister obviously could neither look at nor read the books. She said it was good for her sister to get out. She said, "She is listening to us now, even though she can't hear it."

11 January—The Gloomy Donkeys look as miserable as ever. There are now two of them and a baby in the field. They are something I am now accustomed to, but I still don't like them. What really shocked me the other day was seeing a llama in the next field. Expensive, rare breed French Donkeys are a surprise in Tipperary, but the llama leaves me speechless.

23 January—We came off well with the electricity failure last night. Ours went off at about 10.30pm and returned at 4am. Most of the people in the village and down the valley had no power until one the next day. Some people are saying that swans got mixed up in the wires and that is what caused it. Cables are drooping down everywhere. Wooden fences are falling over. I don't know if that is the wind or the extraordinary amount of rain that has just softened the ground. What could stand up for long in this water? The village now has huge lakes around it. These lakes are full of swans. Maybe they are the swans who are usually in Ardfinnan. Or maybe some are swans and some are geese. A lot of damage is still unrepaired since the heavy winds of last Saturday.

Paddy, up the road, lost the roof off his tool shed. The tin roof blew quite a good way from the building and into someone else's field. All his tools are destroyed. This is the same Paddy who has been going back and forth to Geneva to woo a young Filipino woman. She is a lot younger than himself. They are planning to marry next month in the Philippines.

26 January—Simon took the old car in for its test this morning. All the men in the NCT centre left the other cars they were testing and swarmed all over it. There is a new and concerted effort to get old cars off the road. Once a car passes all the tests for emissions and safety things, they can only pick on small details. A car with more than 300,000 miles on the clock is not just a dinosaur, it is a Major Undesirable. The only things they could find wrong were a headlamp which was somehow less than perfect and the number 8 on the license plate. The top bit of the 8 was filled in with black instead of white. That will be corrected with some white paint, or some white-out, as used for a typewriter.

It seems like a hundred years ago when I took my old Citroën van for inspection. Because it was registered as a commercial vehicle, it was supposed to have very heavy duty tyres on it. The garage where it was being fixed took the appropriate tyres off a Post Office van, and put them onto my van. They told me to hurry right back after the test so that they could replace the tyres on the Post Office van. That was the Old Ireland. The fuss over the filled in number 8 is the New Ireland.

4 February—One thing I have noticed about this New Austerity is the lack of new cars. It used to be a real sign of the New Year and a sign of the prosperity of the country to note all the brand new cars which appeared at what seemed like the very minute that January began. This year I have not seen one single car with an 09 registration. This is a small thing but a telling one. The whole place is falling apart and it promises to get worse. As I listened to the radio yesterday, people were calling in to say what they were giving up as a result of their pensions, or their salaries, or their jobs getting cut. I was shocked to hear that so many were not going to pay for their rubbish removal any more. They say very calmly that they will try to dump it at their workplace or in someone else's bin.

5 February—We stopped in at the bar last night after picking up a delivery of books at the shop. It was about 6 o'clock. We were talking with some people when the pay phone rang. Even with the many mobile phones around, the pay phone gets a lot of use. Coverage for mobiles is a bit dodgy with the mountains, or

just generally in rural areas. Usually when the phone rings, it is someone looking for someone else, so whoever answers calls out to ask if that person is there. If the person is there but doesn't want

 to be found, they just shake their head and the one who answered the phone says no, he or she is not here. Often, it is just someone being beckoned home because their tea is ready.

I was the nearest to the phone, so I answered it. A man asked me if this was Nugent's Bar? He asked if it was Newcastle? He asked if it was County Tipperary? I said yes to all three things. Then he asked me how to get there. I asked him where he was. He said he was in Dublin. I asked the few people present who would want to give directions and John, who lives in France, volunteered. He gave the directions from Trim, in County Meath to Newcastle and then he handed the phone to Christy who likes to be introduced as the Mayor of the village. Christy spends most afternoons sitting in the bar, always on the same stool. Christy asked this man why he wanted to come to Newcastle from so far away. The man said he was coming down to paint the telephone exchange building, and some Eircom men had given him the phone number of the bar in order to get directions.

18 February—I took the little car to have its NCT today. The whole system used to work like clockwork. Today I arrived fifteen minutes early but waited for 25 minutes past my appointed time before my turn. Too many people were crowded into the small waiting room. There are only seven chairs in the room, and they were all full. There were at least six people standing at any one time.

My favourite part is when the inspector takes the money, car details and keys from the next schedualed person and then goes out to fetch their car. He drives around the corner and into the building, tooting the horn as he goes. It is very cheerful. I know they are just testing the horn but I think it makes everyone feel a little happy. Once the car is inside the testing area, there is a lot of revving of the engine. The sound is loud even inside the waiting room. Everyone looks around and raises eyebrows at one another. There are large windows so we can look into the testing centre and see which car is being revved while we wait. Today, one lady repeated six or seven times that her husband would never race the engine like that in a century. She was quite thrilled with the naughtiness of it.

My car failed the test. The young man seemed worried that I was driving away in it. He said that the brakes were extremely dangerous and that he wouldn't let his mother or his sister or anyone in his family drive my car. I drove away, carefully and slowly, and went to the garage to see Mike. He thought maybe it was not as bad as the test man suggested. I left it with him, and he promised to put it up on the lift tomorrow.

19 February—The car is indeed as bad as the inspector said it was. Apparently there is a bit of brake cable that could go in a second. And that is just one of the problems. We have to decide if it is worth it to spend a fair amount to repair a 17-year-old car yet again, or is it better to think about a new car. Old cars are cheap right now. We should really have just one car, but with second-hand cars, it seems one of them is always breaking down. It is difficult because we live in such a car-dependent location. I never had any fondness for this particular motor, so I am not sad to say goodbye to it. I do worry about what to do with all the cassettes we have. That car was the only place left for playing them. It is sad to think of a lot of music that I don't have in any other form. Compilations made over the years by friends and old stuff that I would never buy again, but which I do like to hear every once in a while. Has everyone else just thrown away all their cassettes by now?

21 February—Cold, crisp and sunny today. We sat outside the kitchen door having a cup of tea in the afternoon sun. Staying near feels right. It has been a beautiful spring day, even if it is still only February. The cows started chasing after me as I walked on the track through Joe's fields. They were all so young and frisky and light on their feet. They just rushed along with me for the sake of somewhere to go. A crowd of them raced all the way up to the barn, even though it was a good three hours before their milking time. When I walked through the other Joe's farm on my way back down, another young crowd raced along beside the stone wall and then along the fence following beside me as if wherever I was going was some place to be going.

28 February—Today is the first day this year that I have been outside to hear the Ardfinnan church clock strike six. The wind needs to be in a certain direction for us to catch the sound of the bells. It

was still light and the sky was a bright blue with big pink clouds picking up the dropping sunlight. A beautiful evening. The bells played the Angelus. When watching the news channel at six o'clock, the bells ring and there is a minute of silence, or rather a minute of bells and just silence from the listeners. On the television, we are shown people stopping and crossing themselves and listening to the bells, each with a thoughtful expression on his or her face. On the radio, there is just the sound of the ringing bells. In the bar, people usually stop talking and some of them cross themselves. I am always interested that the sound of the bells usually comes from the TV or the radio, rarely from real outdoor bells. Even as a non-participant, it seems important to be quiet and respectful of other people's silence.

2 March—I received my free seeds and free seed potatoes today from the Irish Seed Savers Association. I have been a member for many years now, but I have never taken advantage of the offer for free seeds each spring. I have had quite a few apple trees at the special member rates. I like getting the old Irish varieties. It feels important to keep planting and growing them. Every year I ask for a Mother of Household which is an old Tipperary apple, and every year I am too late. Every year they plan to graft some more and they promise me one, and every year I have not had one. Yet.

As for the potatoes, I have been reluctant to ask for them because I hate the floury potatoes which are so loved in Ireland. When we were first here, I remember asking a greengrocer about the potatoes he was selling. He said they were wonderful and that they would Explode in My Face. For me, this was not a positive attribute. I like waxy potatoes. Here, waxy potatoes are called Wet, and people sort of sneer when they speak of them.

Most of the potatoes offered by the Seed Savers are of the floury variety, but this year I noticed some Rattes from France and another waxy one called Ulster Sceptre. I could have chosen three kinds, but I had no idea how many free potatoes I would receive. I did not want to be inundated with potatoes to grow. Today I received two little paper bags in the post, each with five potatoes in it. Both of the varieties sent were not the varieties I ordered. Both of what I received are floury varieties. I don't feel too threatened. Ten potato plants will not be an overwhelming crop.

24 March—There are some good things about living in a cold house. It is sometimes hard to remember them when it is really really cold. I always leave a glass of water on the dining table before bed. If I

walk by in the night, the water in the glass is absolutely perfect. Cold and refreshing.

25 March—Michael is a farmer. He lives right in the middle of the village and he does his farming just outside the village. Last week, he was walking his small dog at 9 am and a huge Staffordshire Bull Terrier came rushing out from somewhere and tried to attack his dog. Michael is a tall man, and he is strong. He picked up his dog and held it up over his head with both arms. He kicked the Bull Terrier again and again to try to get it to stop lunging up at his dog. The Bull Terrier clamped its teeth around Michael's forearm and would not let go. Finally he got his own dog's lead wrapped around the neck of the attacking dog. He squeezed and squeezed until he killed the dog. Not many people would be strong enough to do that. Nor would they have the presence of mind to do it.

Michael is now wearing a big bandage on his arm and has been nicknamed The Bohergaul Strangler. He was wearing his rubber boots when he kicked the dog. His foot has been hurting all week. It was like kicking a wall, he said.

2 April—I went to the shop and bought chicken wire and some of the metal stakes that the farmers use for fencing. Simon did not want to do it, but I insisted that we make a small narrow caged area for Em outside her house. We had a few lengths of wooden fencing from our first plan to confine her. The vet originally said she needed an area no bigger than 1 metre 80, so that was what we hoped to provide. Her leg is much worse after the visit from our Japanese friends. She was in high spirits when they came and went right into her most hysterical hosting mode. They threw the rubber sandwich over and over again. She fetched and frolicked and had a grand time. They shouted and complimented her in Japanese and she was delighted with all the attention. They loved it and she loved it and now she can barely walk. We just must fence her in if she is ever going to get better.

We built a pen and put her in it and she looked disgusted to be there. I worked on some weeding and small jobs nearby. I talked to her the whole time and said nice gentle cooing things to make her feel good about it all. She made no effort to escape. After a while I went into the house to get something and within minutes she was in the house right beside me. She had just been humouring me by staying in the pen. Apparently escape was easy. Simon was delighted and very proud of her. I shall have to work harder on this prison.

3 April—I did some errands and stopped at the butcher's shop to get a bone for Em. At one o'clock, when she usually has a small lunch snack, I put the bone into her new cage. She looked at me in disbelief, but I outstared her and eventually she entered the cage and began examining her bone. It was quite a big one, so she was busy with it for an hour or more. I looked out the window often. I congratulated myself on being so clever. She would accept her confinement if it came with the promise of such tasty treats. I could not provide such a fattening incentive every day, but perhaps the mere possibility of a delicacy would convince her to stay put. Some time later, I looked out and saw her wandering across the yard sniffing at bushes. Another escape. This is a badly made cage.

7 April—Every rural place has bathtubs in fields. It is a way to get rid of old tubs and they are useful to provide drinking water for cows. I enjoy a bathtub in the landscape.

9 April—Wild all-day rain today. It started last night with winds. It has not stopped once. Sometimes it is like a billowing cloud of rain, moving to the left and then moving to the right. Some of the time, it is just sheeting down in hard diagonal lines. A lot of the time it is raining sideways.

Simon wanted to continue printing this morning but there is a leak in the shed just above where he stands to print. We tried to figure out a way to deflect the rain, with a hat, with tape or even with an umbrella, but really it is just too miserable to be in a dripping shed while working with paper. His self-imposed schedule for this book is to print two pages a day. He will just have to print four pages tomorrow.

10 April—Today is as lovely a day as yesterday was foul. The countryside has that deep silence about it. Many things are closed as is normal on Good Friday: bars, restaurants, banks, schools,

factories. Farms, of course, keep at the work of farming and some supermarkets seem to be open.

I saw a sign: THERE WILL BE BAG-PACKING IN SUPER VALU ON GOOD FRIDAY AND EASTER SUNDAY IN AID OF SOUTH TIPP HOSPICE.

Bag-packing is a way for various organizations to earn money for their cause or project. At the checkout counter there will be someone wearing a tee-shirt or a hat which advertises their good cause. We hand over our cloth shopping bags to them and they pack up our purchased items. Then we are obliged to put money into their collection can. We, the customers, are a captive audience and I should think such collections are very successful since we cannot really say no to their packing of our groceries, and once they have done so, it is difficult not to pay something in return.

14 April—Dessie has changed the cottage enormously in the year or so since he has been there. Mary Corbett would barely recognize it now. After trying for months to squeeze his car right up close to the stone wall in order to keep it off the very narrow road and doing various things like even clearing off all the ivy to make the most of every teeny bit of space, he gave up. He had a friend knock down some of the stone wall and made himself a muddy parking spot. Then he cleared and made a vegetable patch, which has been covered in manure all winter. For a long time, he kept asking me if I was Canadian, but we seem to have finally got my nationality settled.

Dessie's dogs are all over the road. Often his little dog Titch comes racing out, barking like mad. She leaps out in front of cars. She seems to have a death wish. I have rescued her several times. Dessie told me to just kick her. I said, "No, I don't kick dogs." He said "It's okay. I do it all the time. Just kick her. It's the only thing she understands." I answered that I would not be kicking the dog, now or ever. I said that there are other ways to train a dog.

Now the other dog, which we all thought was a Pit Bull Terrier, is growing up and is much taller and stronger. This is the dog that Dessie gave to his mother and which she gave back to him because she was frightened to have such a dog. It turns out that it is a Staffordshire Bull Terrier, not a Pit Bull. Oscar, a very friendly Labrador from down the way, has been driven away by this dog. I spoke to Dessie about how aggressively the Staffordshire is guarding the whole length of the road. I also asked if he had heard about Michael getting attacked. He had heard, of course, and said maybe he should get a muzzle, because he did not want anyone to be afraid of the dog. He asked if I was afraid and I said yes.

He built a kind of pen for the two dogs with wooden pallets. He swears that the Staff is never out and loose when he is not at home. Twice in this last week, the dog has been out policing the road while Titch, the noisy but harmless little one, is safely locked up. Dessie is not at home, and there is no muzzle in sight. I do not like where this is going.

15 April—We stopped at a restaurant and bakery with a sort of cafeteria line. Halfway down the line there was a huge tray full of dozens and dozens of slices of freshly baked brown soda bread, each slice generously buttered. It did not seem to matter whether someone was buying a cup of tea or a sandwich or a full hot lunch, when the person got to the cash register, the woman there asked if he or she had got their piece of bread. A thick slice of buttered bread came with everything.

19 April—We went to the Farmers' Market in Cahir yesterday. It has been a while since we've been there because we have been attending the Clonmel Market instead. Jim and Keith wanted us to report on what the competition was like. We tried to explain some things, but did not tell them that the organic vegetables are much more plentiful and varied in Clonmel. That would make them sad, because they are the vegetable men in Cahir. We love the friendliness of this market. The small physical space full of friendly people make it a very welcoming place.

There is an older man who only started there last year. He usually has a few boxes of eggs and some potted plants. I asked if he would like me to save some egg boxes for him, if not, I said I would just be putting them onto the compost heap. He said, "Yes, I would be happy to have more boxes if you think to bring them, but both things are nice things to do with an egg box."

I used to take empty jam jars to Mary, the cake and jam lady. After a while she would pick through whatever I had brought and reject any that were not her exact kind of jar. Some days I was leaving with as many as I arrived with, so I have stopped taking them. She doesn't seem to mind. She probably has a shed full of jars by now anyway. When we buy a jar of jam from her, the jar is carefully placed in an empty sugar bag for the carrying home.

This same Mary is a huge fan of Edvard Grieg. She has made

several trips to Norway. These trips are pilgrimages. She goes to sit on Grieg's garden bench and to hear Grieg's piano being played. She knows every piece of music he has written and her eyes light up when she speaks of him.

21 April—I managed to walk past Dessie's without any dog action. I noticed that the pile of rock, soil and rubble, which had been pushed aside for his parking place, is now topped with the back bumper of his car. He had the bumper tied on with string for quite a long time. I am not sure if he just backed into the pile and the bumper fell off or if the string gave out and he threw it there just as a place for it to be.

22 April—I was on my way to the hospital in Kilkenny. I was late and didn't know where the hospital was. I stopped at a petrol station and asked the girl at the counter for directions. She had no idea where the hospital was. A postman came in, so I asked him for directions. He gave me a direct and simple route. Even I could not get lost. I got there on time for my appointment. About two hours later, as I was leaving through the hospital's main entrance, someone tapped me on the shoulder. I was greeted like an old friend. It was the postman. He was pleased that I had found my way and wanted to tell me so.

30 April—I was in Cork today for a few appointments. I try never to visit the city without stopping in to buy two rolls of Silver Mints from the tiny shop on the corner. The old man who runs it is even now the same degree of ancient as he was when I first visited. It is a small, dark and narrow room with sweets, cigarettes and not a whole lot else available for sale. There is often another elderly man inside with him when I stop by. One of them is behind the counter and one is on the customers' side. They pretty much fill up the place. I usually feel that I am interrupting a conversation when I enter, but I also feel that they do not mind the interruption. It is a gloomy place, but I like it. The street outside is changing all the time, with new shops, and building projects and scaffolding as close as right next door. I do not know how this shop has survived and not been squeezed out. It feels nearly invisible with all the rushing

and movement outside its door. I worry that no one goes in. I could buy Silver Mints in any shop. My small, very occasional purchases will not keep the shop afloat.

6 May—Election posters have begun to appear. Distances are long in the countryside. Some people drive a lot and cover a large area in the course of a day but others stay right near their own homes. It is a big job for the politicians and hopefuls to get their name and their face out and about to a widely dispersed audience.

Most posters appear on trees and telephone poles. Sometimes they are stuck into the ground on a stick. My favourite system is the little tent-like structure on a tiny trailer. The trailer is left beside a road somewhere and the two sides of the tent have a poster on each surface so that they can be read from opposite directions. After a few days someone collects the little trailer and drives it to another spot for more exposure. I think the element of surprise works with this mode of advertising because just when you get used to the trailer and its candidate being there, it is gone. You might see it somewhere else, but you might not.

1 June—We sat out in the still warm evening sun with three friends last night. Every once in a while chairs were moved as bits of shade fell upon us. We ate walnuts and then we ate oysters. We drank beer, wine and elderflower cordial, according to taste. The very rectangular and handsome woodpile was nearby. It had a large convex bulge in it. Our friends could not help but notice the bulge and comment upon it. Simon assured them that it was stable. He said that it was three logs deep and not going anywhere, or at least not until the winter when the wood might be dry enough and ready for use. In spite of this reassurance, no one wanted to sit very close to the woodpile. We woke up this morning to find logs all over the grass. The pile had collapsed, or exploded, in the night. It is much too hot to restack it.

11 June—We stopped in at Rose's on our way home. We bumped into Paddy McGarry there and listened to his anger about the changes in the world at large, and more specifically in his world.

He spoke of going out with the dog in the early morning and not hearing any of the starting up sounds of machinery. This, to him, says the most about the absence of work in construction and about the recession biting. The quarries are quiet. His wife is obsessed with the rubbish that is being dumped in the woods. People are trying to save money by any means possible, so they are dumping in the woods rather than paying bin charges or driving to the dump. Since they do not walk there, they do not give a damn. She is very depressed by it all. Her beautiful and peaceful world is being violated.

I am noticing how many men I see walking children to and from school or pushing prams, or in the grocery store with small children in tow. This has not been a weekday sight until very recently.

17 June—I never get this business of call and ring right. When I say to someone that I will call later, I mean that I will telephone but they think that I mean that I will drop by or stop in. They say, "Oh, no need to call. Just give us a ring."

18 June—I drove along the valley road from Clogheen back to Newcastle. At a house near to the turn-off for the Vee, there was a sign saying FUNERAL IN PROGRESS GO SLOW. Lots of cars were parked on both sides of the narrow road near a house, but there was not another house or a hearse or a graveyard anywhere nearby. This must have been the wake. I asked in Newcastle who had died out Goatenbridge way. Rose thought it might be a certain elderly woman, who had been unwell for a long while, but Seamus corrected her and said "No, she can't be dead because she's dead already."

20 June—I have all these things I mean to ask people about. I should carry my list around with me and look at it carefully and choose which person to ask about what. I don't know who to ask about the blinds.

Everywhere there are scalloped blinds in the windows of houses. Sometimes they are a repeat scalloped shape, and sometimes they are a scallop and a wave-like shape together. They never seem to be just straight-edged blinds. They are almost always white, or light-coloured. If the house is a bungalow, the blinds are pulled down to a height about one quarter of the way down the window. This height is repeated in every window across the front of the house. Every blind is at exactly the same height and the line is even all across the house. If the house has two-storeys, the blinds upstairs and downstairs will all be at the same level. I wonder if this is a long decided plan, and if people discuss it among themselves, or if they just do it because everyone else does it. Every house is sporting decorative blinds at the same height. Every house has the same variations of decorative blinds. No one has their blinds up and down at higgledy-piggledy heights. It always surprises me that people care this much to conform. We must be far down the order. We have no blinds.

26 June—Em continues to move well. She is favouring her bad leg only a tiny bit and not too often. We see it early in the morning or when she has been a little too active, with a visiting dog or after pursuing the wild cats who come down the boreen to investigate things here. We are still barricading the sofa at night so that she can't climb up onto it. I think that the half-sleepy push to get up or down from there was an unnecessary strain on the healing ligament. A few more weeks of no walks and then we'll slowly begin to give her more exercise.

Em was very sweet today. I smashed my head coming out too fast from under the lean-to. I fell hard onto the ground, crying and clutching my head. After a few minutes of noisy sobbing, I continued with a quiet cry. I felt her body pressing against mine. She waited very gently for ten minutes or so until I opened my eyes. She had placed her rubber hamburger just beside my face so that it would be the first thing I would see.

28 June—The weather continues to be wonderful. Dessie has got all sorts of things growing on the dry stone wall in front of the cottage. First he had Grow Bags opened and distributed along the top. These are large bags of soil which are made to be split open and used for the growing of tomatoes or whatever. I gather they are planned to have just the right sort of a mixture of soil in them so that there is no need for a transplant to a pot or a bed. I do not know if they have holes in the bottom for drainage or how the excess water gets out. I think they are not designed to be on display. They are just designed to be useful in a particular kind of place. The bright printed plastic is very gaudy lined up along the stone wall, and really there is no need for flowers in them because all you can see is the bag. Anyway, Dessie has had his colourful flowers growing along the wall in these Grow Bags with a black plastic plant pot in between each bag. Just the other day he put long pieces of wood along the sides of each Grow Bag. I don't know if this was

to cover up the noisy-looking plastic or if it was to keep the bags from toppling off the wall.

The back fender of his car is still on the heap of rubble, along with an old gate and lots of roots and rocks. The car without its bumper looks a little naked from behind.

29 June—ALL THE OLD THINGS ARE GONE NOW AND THE PEOPLE ARE DIFFERENT.

We have had this quotation from Jonathan Williams up on the blackboard for more than a year now. I wrote it there at some time in the months after Jonathan died. We were both reading a lot of his work. We were going back and finding favourite bits and discovering new things. We would point out passages or poems to each other as if one person would not find that exact thing unless the other of us made a point of directing them to it. It was a way of feeling that conversation with Jonathan was still happening and that that conversation would continue. I think this was something he wrote about his own father's death. Already I have forgotten its context, but I look up often, re-read it, and I feel time passing.

9 July—The Polish, Latvians and Lithuanians who have been living and working in Ireland for the past few years are always referred to in the news as Foreign Nationals. I am not sure about the reason for this. I do not think that a French or German or English person living and working here is called a Foreign National. In fact, all these people are part of Europe. Maybe the fact that these newer Europeans are still more foreign-seeming and foreign-sounding is why they get a special form of description.

There is a spot beside the river in Cahir where some of the Foreign Nationals regularly gather to drink beer. I think they do some fishing there too. There used to be big piles of empty aluminium drink cans at the base of the wall. Now someone puts black bin liners on a home-made device by the wall and on a Saturday morning when we go to the market and walk along that river path, there are always two bags already full and neatly tied at the top and two more bags fitted into the hanging devices. This may be the same every morning.

The term Foreign Nationals is just a way to clump everyone together since most of us cannot tell the difference between a Polish

person and a Latvian. I understand there are a number of Moldavians living locally too.

13 July—My home-grown potatoes are good. I cannot say that they are the best potatoes I have ever eaten, but they were okay and at least they were not too floury. They had a fine taste and that unmistakable freshness of just-lifted potatoes. I think we probably could have been eating them for several weeks now, but I forgot to check on them. I think I should probably dig them all up now so that they don't rot or get eaten by slugs and bugs. Storing them somewhere cool and dark is tricky. I fear the mice might find them in the shed. I have to think this one through carefully. Once, years ago, we stored three big crates of apples in the barn, before the barn was finished. We were away when the mice found them. They ate every single apple. I do not want to lose my potatoes in the same way.

15 July—I met a woman out walking with her dog today. I did not recognize her and thought she might be new in the area. We spoke a little and I learned that she is not new, but that she has just taken to walking in a bigger loop from her house. I knew of her family and their fields and it was interesting to put her into context. She knew me by sight and she knew our house. She said "Ah, yes, you are the people who live in the house with words on it." I was interested that that is how our house is described.

We have three of Simon's poems lettered on the exterior walls. One of them is now obliterated by ivy, but still, we know it is there. We also have the 22 inch high metal letters of Hotel Metropole going around the corner on the boreen side of the house. We saw these in a skip in Cork many years ago and thought they were too good to go to waste. When a friend was about to open a shop, we tried to get her to create the shop name from some or all of these available letters, but she wasn't interested in the offer. Instead she named her shop Atomic Age. The shop didn't last long, and the letters are still here.

20 July—The intermittent rain is annoying. The sunny moments are beautiful, hot and drying, but the rain is winning and we are all sick of it. Desperate is the word. The Irish do not have 300 words

for rain. They have 'desperate' and 'soft'. There are probably a few more that I can't think of right now, but those are the two most used around here. The farmers are fed up. There is a lot of concern about getting in enough hay and silage to keep their cows through the winter. There is less and less money each time an animal or a pint of milk is sold. Someone told me that a farmer has to sell six pints of milk to earn the price of one pint of Guinness.

21 July—Five days of the joyful Perimeter Walk, and suddenly Em has started to limp a little. Where has this come from? It must be cat-chasing because our walk has been the same, and it is gentle. No walk tomorrow. I shall give her a rest.

We came up from the meadow this evening and stopped to watch a crow climbing up the slates of the roof. It clawed its way up and then slid back down. This went on for quite a few tries. Em got bored before I did and she went inside to have her night-time biscuits. I could not figure out why the bird did not just fly up to the top of the roof, instead of this endless slipping and slipping on the wet slates.

22 July—Maisie's house has been demolished. I walked up there the other day and saw that the slate roof and all the windows had been removed. I thought this meant that the house would be retained and rebuilt. But the entire building is gone now and there are two large piles of rubble off to one side. The rubble was once the house.

Maisie Gleason lived in that house for a long time. I don't know exactly how many years. It was at least forty years but it might have been longer. She was the housekeeper for Tom Cooney's aunt and uncle. When they died, they left Tom the land and the house. He told Maisie that she could stay there for as long as she wanted. When she died a few years ago, she was ninety-three. By the time she died, she had an enormous number of cats living with her. I had the impression that she and the cats lived mostly in the kitchen but I never went inside to verify this. The smell was impossible. I usually spoke to her from outside the kitchen door or from over the gate on the road. When she invited me in, I always made excuses about being in a hurry. The smell of cat pee, both old and new, was overwhelming, even from outdoors. I gag now just thinking about it. When I consider the permeating quality of these smells, maybe it is better that the house was torn down. Still, I feel sad that another old building has disappeared and will most likely be replaced by something ugly.

Thinking of Maisie reminds me of how consistently surprising and interesting it is to be surrounded by women with names like Maud and Maisie, Fidelma and Geraldine, Breda and Philomena. Most of these are the names of saints. They are names that never stopped being in fashion in Ireland. To me these were names that I might find in novels. I did not think I would ever know people with these names. Actually, I never thought of these names at all.

Many years ago we were at Cork airport about to go somewhere, and we realized that my ticket was incorrectly written. It was for a Breda Van Horn, and that name did not match my passport. We phoned the travel agent and asked for an explanation. We hoped for an immediate solution to the dilemma. Her response was "But surely you have a Breda in your house?"

23 July—The newest offer from the world of supermarkets is what is called Border Shopping. For several years now, people from the Republic have been driving over the border into Northern Ireland to shop. Everything there is much cheaper. In the last year, with the British pound dropping and the euro getting stronger, there were buses being hired to take loads of people up from Dublin to Belfast and Newry. Sometimes the buses were free. Everyone returned laden with bargains and savings. Many of the savings were at stores that have branches on both sides of the border. It has become increasingly hard for these businesses to justify the enormous price discrepancies, especially when many of them really like to market themselves as Irish companies. The first sign of change was when certain stores dropped their euro prices to the same level as pound prices for an area as far as 15 miles south of the Northern border. That prompted questions for the rest of the country. If the prices can be lower up there, then why not down here? Now we have this Treat called Border Shopping being offered. And here we are, nearly 250 kilometres south of the border. It does not excuse the rampant inflation of everything else in the Republic, but maybe it is a start. I fear it won't last.

25 July—I painted the new little fence a soft green which is quiet against the long grass. As I was finishing the second coat, and expecting a downpour at any minute, the men from the broadband company arrived to check up on our abnormally erratic signal. The signal has been in and out all week, making us crazy. We thought a man would arrive on Friday but when he did not, we assumed we would have to wait until Monday. Instead, at 6 o'clock on Saturday

evening, three big Land Rovers arrived with great long ladders on two of the vehicles.

There was one Irishman, and four Poles (Foreign Nationals). One of the men went into the house with Simon to check the computer and to attempt to reset the signal. Another one produced a pair of binoculars which were eighteen inches long; the longest ones I have ever seen. He was trying to make sure that our Line of Sight was still working. We receive our signal off Michael Hickey's roof just over the valley into County Waterford. These radio signals bounce all down the country from place to place. We still find it amazing that we can get broadband in this valley.

The Irishman, who was huge, walked around outside chain-smoking cigarettes and two of the Poles came out of the house and started to ask me about finding mushrooms in the area. They said they try to stop in woods and forests on their way home every night to forage for mushrooms. At the very least, they like to get at least enough for that night's supper. They cannot believe that the Irish have so little interest in mushrooming. They said that mushroom gathering is a national activity in Poland. I was pretty useless at directing them to a source. Later, I realized that they must have noticed the copy of *La Cuisine des Champignons en 200 Recettes* which was lying on the table in the big room. That's why they thought I might know where to look.

They managed to get the broadband sorted without using any ladders.

27 July—I went to have my teeth cleaned this morning. The dental hygienist's room is very small. At some point someone cut a rectangular hole into the door. It looked as if it was waiting to have a small window fitted. It has been like this for many years. Now, I think the idea is that the hole is just there for the air. There is a large wall clock leaning against the wall on top of the radiator. When I lie back in the chair, I can tell the time by looking down between my feet. I always assumed that the clock was leaning there just waiting for someone to hang it on the wall. This has also been like this for many years. Today I noticed that the room has been freshly painted and the clock, which must have been removed for the painting, is back in its place on the radiator.

31 July—I've never known exactly what the Pioneers were. I knew that they wore little lapel pins and that they did not drink any alcohol. That is all I knew. Now I know that they are an organization affiliated to the Catholic Church. When young people are about to make their confirmations and communions, they are asked to sign a pledge saying that they will not drink alcohol until they are 18, or 21. (I think it used to be one age and now it is the other.) After that age they have the choice to remake the pledge, which some people do, and some do not. After 25 years' abstinence, a special pin is awarded.

There are regular meetings of Pioneers, but they do not appear to be out and about seeking converts all the time. That is what I thought they did. They are just a church club of like-minded people. The full name is The Pioneer Total Abstinence Association. I assumed that they would never ever set foot in a bar. That is not true. They sometimes join together to make up a team and participate in pub quizzes.

1 August—There are pink rose petals in the bathtub. There is no water in the tub, just a small scattering of tiny petals. The old ceramic inkpot on the narrow shelf has a few Albertine roses and a cutting of honeysuckle in it. I put the flowers there so that they would reflect in the mirror. Now the petals in the empty tub have made another kind of reflection.

3 August—I am not sure if it is just the weather but the service for my mobile phone is worse than ever. We are quite used to not being able to speak or to receive calls here, but usually texts can come and go freely. I tried to send a text today and since it would not go, I kept wandering around, first in the house and then outdoors. Eventually I found myself standing up on the stile at the edge of the field waving my phone back and forth in the air above my head, in the rain. The text did go.

4 August—At about 11.30 last night there was a huge racket outside. Cows were moaning and mooing, and the tearing and chomping of grass seemed louder than ever. We ignored it for a while, but then I looked out the window and saw the yard full

of cows. They had broken out of the field and into the garden. I am not sure if it was a break-out or a break-in. All the cows who were left out in the big field were racing about, charging the fence and making a lot of noise, while the ones in our garden were just eating like mad.

We rang Joe and then we both went out with sticks and torches to try to keep the cows under control. Two of them raced off down the meadow. We could not figure out exactly where they had broken through, so we just tried to contain the group. It was dark and moonless. We were lucky that they were black and white cows because the white parts made them easier to keep track of. I think there were about seven of them up here. They were delighted to be eating bamboo and tansy and the cherry tree.

Michael arrived down the boreen in his truck and eventually Joe appeared across the fields with his tractor. I am always amazed at how many lights there can be on a tractor. It was very exciting. Joe used the tractor to round up the bellowing crowd on the field side of the fence. There was a really hysterical energy out there. The cows started jumping and racing and running in many different directions. Joe's daughter and I went up the boreen and stayed near the gate which Michael had opened. As he drove the escaped cows up towards us, our job was to direct them back into the field. Simon ran down into the meadow and chased the two who were down there up and all around the house and eventually along the track with the others. It was relaxed and chaotic at the same time. I loved it and could hardly go to sleep later because I kept thinking about it all.

This morning, the grass looks as if it has huge polka dots all over it. The heavy hoofs have made a real mess of the wet lawn, and lots of things are chewed over and ravaged, but nothing is completely destroyed. I expected everything to look much worse this morning.

6 August—The woman from the Environmental Health office came down to test the water in our well. She was outraged at the state of the boreen and was convinced that her car has been irreparably damaged by the brambles and branches. She was wearing little white ballet slippers. I did not think she was appropriately dressed for going off into rural places to take water samples. Most people who have wells do not live in the middle of towns. People in the middle of towns do not have wells, but they usually have proper tarred roads and clear access. I gently suggested this to her, but she was not very interested. We had a bacteriological sample taken but decided to forego the chemical sample this year. The cost of the

chemical test has gone from 35 euro to 100 euro. This is a shocking jump in price. Have they not heard of Border Shopping?

10 August—I have just learned that my laundry basket is not a laundry basket. It is an oyster basket. We saw a show on television about the oyster beds in Galway, and the men had the same basket. The baskets are made of some metal alloy, painted dark green, and appear to come in several sizes. Some are tall. The one I have is short. The basket is placed in the water and is heavy enough not to be pushed along by the water when it is empty. All the openness allows the water to flow through it as oysters are dropped into it. When the basket is lifted up, all the water drains out and it is just full of oysters. All this explains why it is a heavier and sturdier laundry basket than any other I have ever seen or used. I am fond of it. Sometimes the weight of it when it is full of wet washing is nearly too much for me. I do like that I can leave it out in the rain and it never rusts. Of course, a plastic one would not rust either and it would be much lighter.

11 August—A beautiful sunny day. We spent a few hours filling the craters left by the invasion of cows. We are lucky that these escapes do not happen more often.

The woman reading the weather on the radio has such a terrible cold that it is difficult to understand what she is forecasting.

15 August—The Wexford strawberry vans are everywhere. The little covered trailers are all along the sides of roads. There is never a car near the trailers, so I guess they are just towed and dropped off there for the weeks of the strawberry season and used during the day as a tiny, open-ended storage place for the strawberries and whatever else is ripe and ready. The little trailers have tiny wheels, often painted white. I don't know if the wheels are just an axle end awaiting a tyre or if these are just extremely small wheels. I do not think they are made for going any distance. Each trailer is white with hand-painted strawberries on the outside, usually just one big berry per side. These painted berries are visible from far along the road. They are not well painted but I enjoy seeing the variations around the area. It would be easy to make a stencil and to have all the strawberries look the same, but each of these strawberries is different from the others, different from the ones on the other sides of the van and different from any strawberries farther down the road. It makes it interesting to keep an eye out for the next berry.

There is often another sign leaning up against the trailer, the table or a tree which uses painted words to offer New Potatoes, Plums or Apple Juice. The strawberries are described visually. Everything else is described with language.

A person sits in a chair beside the little trailer, usually with a book and a small table. If it is raining, there is an umbrella up over the table. I am not sure how many hours the salesperson has to sit there, but on a cold, rainy and miserable day any amount of time would be too long. The salespeople never have a car or a bicycle near the stand so they must all be dropped off and then collected by a van at the end of the day.

17 August—I just found a newspaper clipping I had saved from a few weeks ago. I still marvel about it: "Deliberations in the trial of five men accused of involvement in a 2.28 million euro tiger kidnapping robbery will not begin until next week because several jurors had tickets for last night's U2 concert."

18 August—Driving out in any direction, I see that everybody has something to sell. In some areas, the roads seem to be lined with stuff. Things are outside houses and in lay-bys. Mostly, it is cars and motorcycles being offered for sale. Today I also saw a ride-on lawnmower, several car trailers, and a pair of elaborate gates with gold-painted tops and an electronic opening device. There was also a long white Rolls-Royce being offered for weddings. Actually, I am not sure if the Rolls was being advertised as a service for weddings, or if it was for sale and the seller was suggesting a possible money-making use for a potential buyer.

21 August—I feel like Christopher Robin every time I walk out over the fields wearing shorts and rubber boots. Today we saw the fox as we reached the top corner of the far field. As always, I do not know which of the three of us was more surprised. The fox hesitated and then raced into the woods. Em hesitated too and then she raced to the place where the fox had been. I think that she likes to be sure that he has escaped well before she has any chance of getting close to him.

5 September—We bought a new stove today. This is a huge thing for us. For all the years we have been living here, the kitchen has been in an extended state of temporary. We have used a camping stove and a small convection oven for cooking and everything has been makeshift and quite rough. Most people are shocked by the kitchen, but now that we have started to fix it up, they keep telling us that they feel sad about it changing. Of course, they have not had to live with it. With each change we make, we have to sit back and look at things for a few days before we do more. It is now in a new state of temporary, but the temporary is changing more often. That means that it really is temporary, rather than the temporary that had become permanent. When we bought the stove, the man in the shop gave us an attachment and some small clips for the hose which has to go through the wall and outside to be attached to a gas canister. He held the items in his hand and looked around for a while until he saw a wrinkled paper bag in the wastepaper basket. He emptied a coffee cup and cake wrapping out of the bag and then put our clips into it. He handed over the old bag with a big smile and said "I'm recycling".

13 September—I saw Michael O'Conner today for the first time in months. He was standing outside his house and he saluted as I went past. As always, he was wearing a clean and well-ironed white shirt, a tie with a tie clasp and his navy blue blazer with gold buttons. I stopped to say hello and to ask how he was. He called me American Lady, so I know that he recognized me. Sometimes he does not know who he is talking to. For many years he called Simon "The Australian". Then he was suddenly "The Scotsman".

Michael worked for many years in England. He was in the British army and then he worked in a car factory in Coventry. When we first came here, he used to ride his bicycle down to the village to get his messages and to go and have a pint at Rose's. He would buy ten or twenty scratch cards at a time and sit and study them for hours over a pint of Guinness. Sometimes he would pull up the sleeves of his blazer and show everyone that he was wearing five wristwatches on each arm. He was also prone to pulling up his trouser leg to display a wound or a partially healed scab from a fall off his bike. It was not unusual to come across Michael a long way in any direction from his house. As one approached in a car, he would stop and stand at full salute until the car had passed. These days he does not wander so far from home, and he rarely salutes. He just watches from inside his gate as the world passes..

15 September—I went to the Recycling Depot at Legaun today. I went yesterday too, but they have now decided to be closed on Monday. While I was writing down the new hours on a piece of paper, an old man got out of his car and came over to talk with me. He was the self-appointed guard of the sawmill next door. I do not know where the sawmill men had gone. This man was quite disparaging about the new hours and the new regime at the dump. It is run by the Department for the Environment now and no longer by the county council. As a result, no one is allowed to take anything away that they might find and want from there. He told me of an angle grinder he had found a few years ago. He took it home and replaced a spring or a coil and then it worked like a dream. He did not have much use for an angle grinder but he was happy to have it just the same. Then someone told him that the Garda needed 193 guns cut up. These were guns which had been seized and which had no legal right to exist in the country. They paid him to destroy the 193 guns with his angle grinder. A Garda stood on duty to ensure that each of the guns was rendered unusable.

16 September—The discussions about swine flu appeared to have gone quiet. We are not being overwhelmed by swine flu in the newspapers or on the radio or television. There are a lot of little bottles of disinfecting hand cleaner scattered about but the subject seemed to have settled down.

Now, suddenly there is a new problem. When people go to a funeral or a wake, at a certain moment the priest suggests that everyone make a demonstration of peace with their neighbour. At this signal, everyone in the church, all of whom are standing, are supposed to turn and shake hands with each other, and with everyone sitting both in front of them and in the row behind them. With the possibility of swine flu, to not shake hands is to appear to be unchristian but to shake all those hands is tantamount to a death wish. A whole new reason for panic needs to be confronted.

22 September—The Polish shops in the area seem to move about a lot. I am not sure if this is about short-term leases, but sometimes there are three or four of them in Clonmel and then for a while

there will be only one. The Polish and Lithuanians like to have their own foods and there is a big business importing these things. I am a big fan of the Lithuanian breads and of the gherkins. They seem to carry everything from magazines to meats, and biscuits to salt. Practically everything is being imported, so that home does not seem so far away. Most supermarkets carry a selection of Eastern European foods now too.

One shop that has lasted for quite a long time already is just outside the West Gate in Irishtown. It is called CHANCE or CHANGE. I am never sure which name is correct. The letters are hand-painted on the wall above the windows on both sides of the corner location. The letters are about fifteen inches high, painted in dark red with a black shadow outline. I often intend to go in to ask what the name really is, but I have decided for myself that it is CHANGE. The shop used to be an equestrian supply shop and its windows were full of saddles and boots and horse feeds. Later it became a bridal shop, with windows full of fluffy white dresses and various bits of wedding paraphernalia. I liked that it had gone from Bridle to Bridal. That is enough reason for me to call it CHANGE.

14 October—The new house just after the corner turn-off towards Neddans has been painted again, but not finished, again. For a long time it was just a gray, cement-coloured house. I fully expected that it was going to stay that way.

Some years ago I overheard two women discussing one of them's newly built house. One woman asked the other if they were planning to paint the house, or would they just leave it 'natural'? To me, there is nothing natural about concrete. The colour of wood may be called natural, but not concrete.

Anyway, this house was gray (natural) for a long time. Then it was painted white up to a certain height. I could not decide if the reason for it not being completely covered with white paint was that they had run out of paint, or if the ladders were just not long enough to go up into the gable ends. It stayed half painted white for six or seven months. Now it has been painted yellow but the yellow stops before the white stopped, so now it is a three-coloured house. I am interested to see how this develops.

16 October—Marianne has a light which is attached to a head band. It is the kind of light that people use when they are exploring caves. She uses it to go into the garden at night to catch slugs and snails.

This might be a good idea for me; the torch, not the slug-hunting. It would improve my night-life.

17 October—Everyone at the Farmers Market was a little bit nervous today because the Health Inspector Lady was going around with a man and a clipboard inspecting everyone for cleanliness and adherence to hygiene rules. The cheese lady said that the Inspector is very stern and critical when she is on duty. Most weeks, she just comes to the market as a regular person doing her shopping.

The woman who makes the various pâtés has the most attractive and clever method for keeping everything chilled. She fills brown balloons with a small amount of water before knotting them. When they are frozen they appear a bit fuller and more solid, about the size of a small fist. As the market progresses, they get limper. The mass of balloons together is beautiful. Her various bowls of mushroom, liver, and fish pâtés sit nicely in the nest of balloons, and the brown is a beautiful colour. I do not think that I have ever before seen brown balloons.

19 October—Suddenly the rose beside the lower barn has begun to blossom. Throughout our miserable wet summer, we have had very few roses. Now, as the nights get colder and the days get shorter, this plant has decided to make up for lost time. It is a climbing rose which I bought as a gift for Simon eight years ago. It has well-formed blooms, cream-coloured and edged with deep pink. Ordinarily the flowers are freely produced over a long season. Not knowing a great deal about roses, I bought it because it was called Handel, and at the time we were obsessed by Handel's 'Where'er you walk...'. We were listening to it over and over again. For some reason which I do not understand, we have since taken to calling that rose the Edward Elgar, and neither of us ever remembers that we have the wrong composer in mind. I guess we have changed the name of the rose.

We have another climbing rose which is even more prolific but whose blossoms last for only a day or two. That one is on the side of the barn with the grass roof. It is one of the few plants that was here when we arrived. I have been told that it was

a favourite of Kathie English, who lived her whole life in this house. I have tried hard to keep it healthy for her. This rose is a soft pink and it has a sweet sweet smell. This is the Albertine. It too has had a bad summer.

27 October—It is a wild, rainy day. Again. Everything is blowing and gusting. At the shop, a woman announced: "This weather is so bad that if you hang a wash, you nearly need to be standing there beside it." She was obviously the kind of woman who ran to bring her washing in if it started to rain. She assumed that we were all obsessed enough to rush back into the house with our wet clothes. I have left mine out on the line for days. Nothing seems to dry wherever it is anyway.

We have some old horrible towels which I put down on the rugs when Em comes in from outdoors during extended wet weather. Her first act is always to throw herself down on a rug and to begin to clean herself. The towels on top of the rugs keep the rugs vaguely cleaner, but the towels themselves are horrible to see. One of them used to be a gold colour and the other one used to be green. They are now both faded and gray and filthy-looking, even after they have been washed. We get used to having them down on the floor, and we walk over them as though they are the normal floor covering.

No matter how muddy and wet she gets, Em always cleans herself perfectly. We frequently receive compliments about her beautiful coat. Sometimes I am asked what sort of shampoo we use on her. No one believes that we only ever wash her if she has rolled in something exceptionally disgusting and smelly. She is an obsessive self-cleaner.

28 October—It was a beautiful, blue sky day today. I had to go to town to the doctor, which was a bit of a pity because I would have loved to be out in the garden. As much as I dislike sitting in the waiting room with its ratty magazines and noisy television set, I enjoy seeing my doctor because we always have interesting conversations. The first time I went to her office, she stood up when I entered the room. She sang me a song in

German in a sweet but quavery voice. It was a song about the flower Erica growing in the mountains. On finishing the song, she sat down. She had never met anyone named Erica, so felt she just had to sing that for me. She only knew one song in German, and that song had my name in it. Since then we have been good friends.

My doctor's current worry is about her impending retirement. She does not want to retire because she loves her work and loves keeping abreast of new medical developments and challenges. She hates the idea of missing anything. Her sister, who was another kind of doctor in Dublin, retired a few years ago. The sister was at a bit of a loss for a while and then began to work as an extra in films. She has since become addicted to the very early morning starts on a film set, and to the hours of waiting around for one's little bit of an appearance. The sister enjoys the community of people on the sets and she loves finding out what all of them did before they came together for that particular movie. My doctor feels reassured by this and now trusts that her own retirement will open up a new world for her too.

29 October—There are huge piles of wood, pallets and junk in various fields. The piles have begun to get bigger and bigger in the last few weeks. These are for the Halloween night bonfires which will be lit all over the countryside in the darkness. They will be accompanied by fireworks. Everywhere is so wet, I wonder if any of the fires will even light. Yesterday was dry, but I think a week of sunshine might not be enough to dry the land and the wood.

We have our own wet weather problem. The new (used) car we bought in the spring was inexpensive and did not have many miles on it. Our mechanic friend told us that it was a good brand and that it was cheap because the Irish do not like the Seat brand. He said it is in the Volkswagen family and that it is a good car, just unpopular here. I thought the car an ugly shade of green and hated the name Ibiza, but the price was right. We did not think to ask why people here do not like the Seat. Now we know. When this car goes through deep puddles and the distributor gets wet, the car loses power until it is forced to stop. The car will not start again until the distributor has had time to dry out. This has happened twice and both times the car had to stay overnight down in the village until it was ready to drive again. It is crazy to live down an old rough boreen which has lengthy and deep puddles in multiple locations after every heavy downpour. Heavy rain is not a surprise here. It is crazy to own a car that we cannot drive in the rain. This car is made for Spain.

2 November—I took the evening meadow walk with Em in amazing bright moonlight. I think the moon is full. I turned off the torch and the night was so bright that we ran down and back up the paths in perfect blue/yellow light. Was it blue or was it yellow? It was bright and eerie at the same time. I am not sure what colour it really was. It was beautiful, mostly because it had been bucketing with rain less than thirty minutes earlier. The whole day has been like this. Horrific heavy rain and then bright skies and dancing clouds. Tonight we had the rushing clouds in the bright moonlit sky, and now, as I write, the rain is lashing down on the roof again.

5 November—TJ, the blacksmith, has a brand new trailer out beside the road. It is chained to the gate with a lock and a sign saying FOR SALE. It is his usual sort: an open trailer welded of strong metal. The outside is painted blue and the inside is painted a rich rusty brown-red. Most people around here know that TJ makes trailers and most people who own a trailer have one of TJ's trailers. We all know where he lives so anyone who wanted a trailer would just go by and talk to him. I have never seen one out on display like this. This is another sign of Hard Times and things for sale by the road.

6 November—Dance bands were very popular here in the fifties and the sixties but if they were trying to earn money playing the dance halls, they had to leave the country during Lent since no dancing was allowed. They would book themselves into the dance halls of Britain or even the United States. Some of them did so much better there, that they never came back. Some came back much later, when they were famous.

7 November—The sound of ceaseless rain is driving me mad. The ground is soggy and the teasels are falling over. The grass is a brilliant shade of green and it is still growing. Everything is conspiring to make the wetness as unpleasant as it can. I looked into the cupboard under the bed and saw my old black and white photograph of Le Sommeil des Mages on the inside of the door. It is a twelfth century carving from the cathedral in Autun. I love it. I made several painted versions of this piece years ago. The three sleeping kings are shown sort of piled up on top of each other. I enjoy seeing this photograph inside my cupboard. I have several things on the inside of doors so that I can find them when I am looking for something else. I put an old chart of Nuts and Bolts on the inside of Simon's clothes cupboard door. I think it is from the

1920s. The drawings are simple and everything is divided into categories for easy reference: Special Bolts for Common Uses. Washer Types and Detail. Expansion Shields and How to Measure. Etc. I don't think that Simon ever looks at it, but I do. These are the small things that cheer me as I live with this rain.

19 November—It is hard to talk about the hugeness of this rain and the devastation everywhere. I can see the news and listen to the radio but really, I can only see what I see here. Any place else is not really real. I have heard it reported that this is the worst rain and flooding for two years. It is the worst rain in living memory. It is the worst rain for 24 years. It is the worst rain for a thousand years. Everyone is trying to define how bad it is. We have neither lost electricity, nor our water supply, as so many people have. We are sitting high and dry. The news of bridges collapsing and being closed sounds terrifying. The power of rushing water is hard to believe. Thousands of people have been evacuated from their homes and thousands of cattle and sheep are stranded. One man on the radio today spoke of an area near the Shannon where 60,000 acres of farmland are underwater. I cannot picture 60,000 acres. That is just one example. Ireland is underwater. As I walk out, I examine the places where the road has been ripped away. Gravel and tar and stones were just gouged out of the road and huge long and deep gashes remain. Subside and submerge are oft-repeated words.

23 November—There appears to be a new version of supermarket shopping. I think it is another sign of Hard Times. Very few people take a trolley, or even a small wire basket. They walk around with as much as they are going to buy in their arms, or else they buy only as much as they can carry. I think this is a form of self-regulation.

1 December—Carmel told me that an old house can't be knocked down unless the chimney has fallen. People who want to build a new house on the site of an old one will often go to the site and knock the chimney a bit to ensure that permission for a new house will be granted. A falling down chimney means that it is okay to tear down the rest of the house.

3 December—The geese are flying by, heading south in huge flocks. The noise is often so loud that I rush outside to see them. It is just too big a sound to ignore. Every time it happens, it is exciting. And every year it is exciting all over again. Em barks and races along underneath what looks like a thousand geese.

9 December—The oil men came down to fill the tank with heating fuel. We have turned on the heat only in the last few days. We hate to start the heat because it heralds the real beginning of winter.

Old houses used to be desirable with their character and drafts and idiosyncrasies. Now they appear more and more like obsolete monsters. A well-designed energy-efficient house feels pretty warm and very enviable on a cold day. Some friends living in an Envelope House use a single piece of wood to heat the whole house for an entire day.

Of course, if we had one of those wonderful houses we might not see our friendly oil men. Because our boreen is too narrow for a normal oil truck, we used to get a mobile tank delivered. The tank would be left here and Simon would pump it all out and into our tank by hand over a few days. Then he would take the empty tank back to the oil company in the Nire Valley. After a while, we found someone else who had a mobile tank that could be plugged in to our electricity, through a window, and the pumping out was much easier. Now the tank is brought on a small truck and it has its own generator. The pumping out and into our tank is simpler still.

The delivery continues to be made by two men, and we always invite them in for tea and biscuits. They like having tea and a chat, and I wonder if that is why the two of them come together. They say that they rarely have tea with anyone these days because no one is at home when they deliver. Everyone is out at work. They are complimentary about our tea because the water from our well has no chemistry in it. It does make a lovely cup of tea. They are not the only people to comment favourably about our tea.

We sat and talked about many things. One of the men, John Joe, lost his wife last year. We discussed that and we discussed the predictions for this afternoon's Budget. John Joe always wears a tie and a white shirt underneath his zip-up oil man suit.

I offered two kinds of biscuits and pointed out that one kind was a ginger biscuit. I have noticed that a lot of older people here do not like ginger biscuits, even if they are coated with chocolate. I mention the presence of ginger ever since Tommie took one bite and left the rest of his biscuit balanced on the table edge. He never said a word but he has been skittish about any biscuits offered here since. John Joe and Ned loved the ginger biscuits and they loved the almond biscuits. They did not even mind that we had no proper milk and that we gave them soya milk in their tea. When they left, they thanked us for the Christmas Party.

11 December—Today is the one year anniversary of Em's imprisonment for the healing of her cruciate ligament and the imposition of the strict diet. To look at her now, it is hard to remember that terrible limp. It is easy to remember her as a fat dog, though, because we have so many photographs of her like that. People were always very diplomatic, in ironic kind of ways. They might have said "She's a well-fed dog" or "She has no trouble with eating her dinner" or "She will not be after wasting away any day soon". Now that she is so slim, she moves better and more youthfully and some people even think that she is a new, younger dog. That is a great compliment, but I am very glad that she is the same dog. There is no sign of the limp. She runs and races and chases and swims happily, and all with ease.

12 December—I was in the supermarket looking for tea. Everything had been moved and nothing was where it used to be. I asked a boy who worked there where the tea had gone. He directed me to the biscuit section. He said, "It's only logical. Sure, you wouldn't want a cup of tea without a biscuit, now would you?"

19 December—When we go to the supermarket before Christmas, there is always one day, like today, when we are greeted by someone from a charitable organization who gives each customer a big brown paper bag. The idea is that while we are doing our own shopping, we will also buy some things for more needy people. The person giving out the bags suggests the things that might be useful and appreciated. When we leave the check-out, we each separate our purchases and put the things to be donated into the paper bag. On the way out of the store, we hand over our bag full of food. I have never seen this particular system in action anywhere else.

23 December—I saw Dessie as I walked around today. He has been off doing a course in Limerick for a few weeks. In his absence, his sister has been feeding his new cat. When he set off for the course, there were four huge bags of kitty litter on the windowsill in the porch. I watched them disappear one by one over the weeks. Now they are all gone and Dessie is back home. We talked about his fine new spacious driveway which is covered in gravel and has room for several cars. He said "Yes, isn't it sad that I waited a year for this space and now, I'll be leaving."

He has been offered a house over near Burncourt with more space for gardening, so he'll be moving soon. All the very substantial fencing he made to keep the dogs contained has been designed to be removed and taken with him. The fences were made by taking apart old pallets and reusing the timber boards. Some of the fence lengths have elaborate curved tops. These curvy bits are covered with white plastic. Dessie explained that this covering was made by slicing open electric cable piping. The reason he put it on the top of his fencing is not for the decoration but to keep the water from soaking into the end grain of his fence. The opposite piece of the fence, the piece he cut off to make the curve, is lower down on the ground so that from his window he sees two wavy horizons topped with white.

24 December—Heavy snow began last night and continued through this morning. Everything is white and new and beautiful. We have never seen so much snow in the twelve years we have lived here. We dropped every plan for the day and put on our boots and walked the three and a half miles to the village. Almost no cars were about and there was that lovely snow stillness in the air.

We made a few holiday visits and deliveries. We did errands for some older people who dared not go out. Then we had a drink at Rose's. We talked with Patsy Tom about the turkeys and chickens which he used to raise and sell every year. He stopped doing it because his hip was bad and he said that there was nothing in it because the price of the feed made the birds too expensive for anyone to buy. We were sorry about this because we always found his chickens so delicious. He was disgusted when we said that we are planning to eat fish on Christmas Day. We are delighted with our fresh fish from the farmers' market. We have fish for the 24th and fish for the 25th. What could be nicer? Everyone here eats both a turkey and a ham on the 25th. There is absolutely no exception to this unless perhaps you are alone, or maybe just two people, and then it is acceptable to have a chicken instead of a turkey. This conversation in the mid-afternoon in the pub was unusual. Everyone appeared to have slowed down. Instead of rushing about because Christmas is coming, people seem to have decided that it is already here.

The walk back home was uphill. It was slower and slippery. The wind was colder and it was against us. We were invited in for a hot whiskey about a third of the way up the road. The house we went into had six big naked turkeys unwrapped and in a pile in the small porch. They were to be delivered later to various family members. Em sat near to the turkeys sniffing carefully, but she did not lick or chew at them.

The hot whiskey helped us with the final push home in the darkness and the swirling snow. Em rushed right into the house and ate her supper at top speed, before collapsing into a heap of sleep.

2 January 2010—The weather woman spoke tonight of snow and storms impinging on the north-west coast of the country. I was surprised to hear her using the word impinge like that, so I went to look it up. The dictionary defines 'to impinge' as to strike or to encroach. It still seems an oddly formal word for an impending snowstorm. There is a lot of language here that sounds to me as if it comes from another time. People often use the word avail: There is a new fruit and vegetable shop in town and you should be sure to avail of its many choices. This is not a word I ever heard in everyday conversation until I came to live in Ireland. I am glad that there are so many surprises.

6 January—With all the snow on the ground, everything looks different. We are used to seeing our lives here against a constant backdrop of bright green. I was looking out at the barn today and noticing the smattering of white which is spread over its stone walls. This white is the remnants of a lime wash from long ago.

When Tom Browne was working on the barn, he took out a small window which was in the centre of the wall and just under the roof. We had decided that we did not need this window. Tom filled the space with stones. He worked hard to make certain that the stone work fitted in with all the stone work around it. It bothered him that the stones he used had none of the lime residue that was on the rest of the wall. I was told to take a little white paint, on a sponge, and to dab it carefully over the new stones so that they would blend with the others around them. He said not to use too much paint. I promised that I would do it the very next time I had the paint out for another job. It is years ago now and I have still never done it.

Tom Browne now sits in a wheelchair in the Cottage Hospital after his many strokes. He has been there for several years. As I look at the barn and see the white of the snow and the white of the old lime wash, it all looks beautiful together. The area where I never added the paint stands out a mile. Maybe it is only me noticing this. Tom would have spotted it right away. Tom Browne always had an eye for detail.

8 January—Our pipes are frozen. We have been expecting it for so long that it is not really a surprise. The surprise is in how much of an inconvenience it is. A milk churn full of water was delivered from the farm above. We have the churn standing in the kitchen with a ladle hanging inside it. We have calculated that it takes exactly twelve ladles of water to make a pot of tea.

10 January—The pipes are still frozen. Greg and Breda walked from their house pushing a wheelbarrow with two large containers of water for us. It was good of them to do this. The trip took them an hour because the road is so icy. On a normal day, it would take twenty minutes to walk from there to here. We still cannot drive in or out of the boreen.

We brought in a few more loads of firewood. There are always

two piles stacked on either side of the wood stove. Now we have made large extra stacks at either end of the sofa, just so that they are warming and drying in advance of us needing to use them. The cold from outside is so deep within the wood that the piles are still radiating cold after several hours. It is too cold to sit on the sofa at all now. The house is not so warm, so maybe this is no surprise. Our refrigerator broke at the beginning of December, but it has been so cold, both inside and out, that we have not yet needed to replace it. For quite a while we were bringing the gas canister for the cooking stove in every night so that it would not freeze, but we gave up on that and now we just use the Rayburn for cooking.

12 January—The water is working again. A torrential rain came and melted all the snow and most of the ice. It provided enough of a thaw to convince the well to start flowing again. I met an elderly man who was walking along carefully with his stick for support. He was cheerful. He said, "Isn't this a fine variety of weather we are having!"

13 January—It seems impossible, but Ireland is running out of water. All through the deep cold, people tried to stop their pipes from freezing by leaving their faucets running. I do not know if the faucets were left just dripping or if they were on full force. This excessive use has been exacerbated by many burst pipes within the system. These leaks are added to the already old and leaky pipes of the various water supplies. Quite a number of city and county councils have been both begging and demanding that people stop leaving their water running. They are asking everyone to reduce their water use in as many ways as possible. None of the requests and orders have achieved much, so now the town water is being turned off from ten at night until sometime in the morning.

As I write this, I am reminded that no one speaks of faucets. What I call a faucet is called a tap here.

16 January—Several places locally have signs out front advertising Dental Repairs. These are often houses in the middle of the countryside. I presume there is a workshop in a shed or in a spare room. If the sign reads While U Wait, there must be a waiting area where the person in need of repair can sit quietly while they wait for their dentures to be fixed. Maybe some people drop off their teeth and return later to collect them. Maybe they have a spare, older set at home or maybe they are happy to spend the day toothless.

I never see one these repair places without thinking of an arranged meeting with elderly friends at a pub some years ago. They wanted to buy us a lunch in order to thank us for something we had done. They thought it would be more special if we ate out somewhere. Mostly, I think the woman was longing to be somewhere other than at her own table for a change. She was longing to eat some food which she had not prepared herself. The food was the usual sort of fare. There was some kind of roast meat and roast potatoes and boiled potatoes and mashed potatoes, along with a selection of overcooked vegetables.

While I sat stunned looking at the enormous mound of food on my plate, the wife nudged me. She wanted to explain why she was removing her teeth and placing them in her handbag. She wanted to explain before the teeth were out of her mouth. She said that the local man who did dental repairs charged too much, so her son had done her repairs for her. He had used Super Glue, which I am sure was never intended to be inside a human mouth. Her son did a thorough job. She was delighted with the repairs and the money saved, even though she now has to take her teeth out before she can eat anything at all.

17 January—There is a piece of white cardboard beside the petrol pumps in the village. It is nicely printed by hand in clear big black letters. At the top of the card are the words EMERGENCY NUMBERS. It lists all the telephone numbers one might need for the Fire Brigade, the Garda, local doctors, and the ambulance. The first number on the list is for the priest. Things have changed a lot in this country and the population's relationship to the church has changed enormously, but in certain kinds of emergencies, I guess the priest is still the first man to ring.

18 January—Em has taken to Walking the Houses. Tommie always used the expression Walking the Houses. He would come up here when we were away and he would take long and purposeful strides as he walked around each building. He was checking to be sure that all the doors were shut and all the windows were unbroken and securely closed. He was checking to see that all was as it should be. He once demonstrated exactly how he Walked the Houses. He wanted to let me know that he took his responsibility seriously.

When Em Walks the Houses, she goes only around this house. She sniffs at everything all along the way, and inspects the bird feeding areas to see if anything good has dropped down to the ground. Sometimes she races fast all around the house, stopping for nothing and looking at nothing. Other times she runs fast, barking like mad and turning her head this way and that as she goes. I like looking out of a window and seeing her rush past. This is all quite new behaviour. It is just since the deeply cold weather. She does not circle the barns in the same specific and choreographed way. Throughout the day she rushes around a lot in all directions, down the meadow and out into the big fields, so all areas are covered, but it is not the same. It is not Walking the Houses. It is just Walking the House.

19 January—Three nicknames, in common usage, which I never heard before I came to live here: Mossie, Toss and Batt. They are short for Maurice, Thomas, and Bartholomew.

23 January—Last night we went down to Rose's for an early drink. By 7.15, the whole place was filling up with people in anticipation of the big rugby match. Munster was playing someone in a final. I have forgotten who it was already, but it was big and important. A load of local people had gone off to the actual match in Limerick. We said hello to a lot of people as we finished our drinks and prepared to leave.

The pre-game discussions were already up on the television screen, as was the little white outline drawing of a pint glass in the bottom right-hand corner of the screen. I always look for the glass. Rose had told us about this little drawing a while ago. If a pub or a restaurant has a subscription to Sky Sports, this little icon comes up on the screen when the station is being aired. Its presence means that the venue has paid its Special Entertainment Charge. Without paying the fee, which I understand is high, the venue has no right to be showing the station. The idea is that the venue is probably raking in money with the extra audience who come to watch the match. A spy, or inspector, for Sky Sports can walk into any bar during a sports event and if the little white pint glass is not on the screen, they will fine the bar. To get around the punitive fines and exorbitant charges, I understand some landlords have taken to painting the pint glass onto their own screen with Tipp-ex. Somebody has even designed a tiny stencil to make it easier for those people who might not be good at drawing.

25 January—The Public Service Announcements come on the local radio station at regular times. I used to wonder how everyone knew exactly when someone had died. I assumed there was an amazing network of people telephoning each other with the news. Every time there is a removal, the street in front of the church is full of people well before the hearse arrives. Eventually, I learned that everyone listens to Tipp FM at a certain time. The name of the person and where he or she died is read, then there is an added note of the townland from which the person originally came. For married

women, the maiden name is read too, so that the family she came from can be known. Sometimes the visiting hours are at a funeral home, but often they say "She will repose at home until being taken to the church, for arrival at 7pm." I am especially fond of the expression "She will repose at home". People can go to pay their respects at the funeral home, or they can just go to the person's own house, or they can await the arrival at the church. A lot of options are implicit in the very brief radio announcement. In the village here, the funeral is always the next day, and it is always at 11am.

29 January—Em and I walked around this morning in howling wind. Each time I reached a turning or a rise in a hill or a dip in the land, I expected the force of the wind to drop. I thought that instead of me striding against the wind, it might hit me from a different side and maybe even push me along from behind. No such luck. It was against me the whole way. Even Em seemed to be struggling with it, and she is a lot closer to the ground than I am. When I looked back to see her straggling far behind me, I put on the big, gruff voice that I only ever use to demand Give Me That Stick! This is my trick to make her accelerate. It works every time. It works if she is far in front of me, or if she is far behind me. It works only if she is carrying a stick. Today she had a small stubby stick which looked like a cigar coming out the side of her mouth. She picked it up as we left the yard and she carried it the whole way without ever once being distracted into dropping it.

Later, I heard that the winds had been so strong in Cork that the B had been blown off the sign for the Butter Museum.

30 January—A long time ago, we all filled in forms down at Nugent's. It was some kind of promotion by Guinness, and Rose was eager to get as many forms completed as possible. It would somehow reflect well on her pub to show that she had a huge crowd of customers. I did not want to fill one in because I do not even drink Guinness, but she said that did not matter. Everyone filled them in and some people filled them in for other people who were not there, or for other people who could neither read nor write. Everyone was promised a free pint

just for filling in the form. As a result of this form-filling, we have received mailings from Guinness ever since. At Christmas there is notification of a free pint in the post. This summer was the 250th anniversary of Guinness, so the printed note said: "Erica! There is a free pint of Guinness Draught waiting for you in Nugent's." At the time coming up to our birthdays, there has always been a card which reads: "A Birthday Pint Waiting for You at Nugent's!" Simon always has my pints as well as his own.

A lot of older men have been rushing into the bar this month, complaining to Rose that they never received their Christmas Pint from Guinness. Another sign of the new Austerity. I suppose the Birthday Pints will disappear too.

9 March—Em and I went up the boreen today. We saw a few cars parked outside the old graveyard at Tullaghmelan. It is a narrow bit of road and it is almost impossible to both park and to be off the road. It is unusual to see even one car there. We continued walking. Just as we reached the gate for the llamas' meadow, a hearse came around the corner, very very slowly. I held onto Em as it passed. It is normal here for people to stop what they are doing and to stand quietly to watch a funeral procession, crossing themselves as the hearse goes by. I am not Catholic, so I do not cross myself, but I thought it polite to stand quietly as the motor passed. I was not expecting 38 cars to follow the hearse. I stood there and Em stood there and every person in every motorcar passed very close to us on the narrow road. I could have touched each car without even stretching my arm out straight. Instead, I had to wave or nod to each car and its occupants, as they all waved and nodded to us. Every face lit up at the sight of Em.

The llama, behind us, was in a state of high excitement. It is rare for so many cars to pass. He raced back and forth like a mad thing. It took a long time for the vehicles to pass because they were driving so slowly. The llama did several lengths of his meadow, and I ended up kneeling on the grass, nodding and waving and holding Em just by resting my non-waving hand on her back. Most of the people in the cars were older, which perhaps explained their delight with Em. Even without seeing them, I would have known that the person being buried in the old graveyard was elderly. There are never any new graves dug unless there is already a family plot. I have no idea how all the cars would have parked up there. The road was just blocked until the burial service was complete.

17 March—We have spent the day ignoring the fact that it is St. Patrick's Day. The post office and the banks and the schools are shut. It is a national holiday. Every year it gets bigger and bigger and more and more international. It is not even a day any more. I have heard it called the St. Patrick's Week Celebration. The large towns have huge parades and there are groups from all over who come to participate. The State Troopers from Massachusetts have a large contingent in Limerick. Who is maintaining law and order during the floods, wild winds and devastation in Massachusetts in their absence? In Dublin, there is a brass band from Switzerland, and there are baton twirlers from Texas, and gymnastic teams from Japan. In Tipperary town there is a Bacon and Cabbage Ceili. In Clonmel, a jug of water will be carried from St. Patrick's Well to the altar of a church in town for Mass.

These are just a few of the things about which I know. Without trying to find out about any of it, the information just gets into my life. There used to be small parades of tractors and scouts and teams and homemade floats in small villages. Of course some of these still exist, but they are mostly eclipsed by all the big stuff. I liked it best when it was little and local.

22 March—Against my better judgment, I have become fond of the llama in his field. I still think it is unnatural for a llama to live in Tipperary, but I have taken to stopping and talking to this llama as I pass. He runs to greet me when I call, so I feel that he knows my voice. This is probably false. He might just run towards any voice. His eyes are very sideways on his head. He turns his head this way and that as if trying to look in the direction of my voice.

I have spoken to him about how disturbed I am with his presence in a meadow in Tipperary. I have talked to him about his isolation. I have described The Gloomy Donkeys who were in this same meadow before he arrived. More recently, I have been talking to him about Peru. I do not know much about Peru, but I fear he knows even less than I. I mention words like Lima, and the Andes and Macchu Picchu because I feel these words are in his brain somewhere. I mention authors like César Vallejo, Carlos Castaneda and Mario Vargas Llosa. I keep meaning to look up things about Peru so that I can tell him more.

I was talking to Breda about this lonely llama. She told me that there is a field not far from here with a whole herd of llamas, but this llama had to be moved away from the rest because he is so bad-natured and he is a danger to the others. This changes my feelings a little. This is a lonely llama with a bad reputation. I still worry that he is lonely, but I am glad that I have never tried to pat him. I was never certain that he would not bite. Now it seems certain that he will bite.

25 March—A bright morning turned into a wet and windy afternoon. I put on full waterproofs and went for a walk, without Em, at the end of the afternoon. Once I was outside, it was much less horrible than it sounded from inside the house. I looked around in the old orchard up at Johnnie Mackin's. There are more daffodils out up there than there are down here. The ground under the apple trees is covered with wild garlic. The smell as I walked about was lovely. I filled my pockets with handfuls of the leaves. This is foraging. Foraging is the new word. Foraging is fashionable. I read it everywhere. Menus do not just mention a herb like mint. They announce that the mint has been 'freshly foraged'. I do not think that you can walk out into your garden and pick some mint and call it foraging. If you knew where that mint was and if you were probably the person who planted that mint, you are not foraging. You are just picking. You might call it harvesting but even that is a stretch.

6 April—Wild winds and rain all night. I kept waking up to the sounds of the gales. Today there is water everywhere. Every field has puddles and ponds. I am surprised that there is not more destruction visible after the strong winds. The water streamed down the boreen all morning as if it was part of a river and not simply running down a rough road. As I write, it is afternoon and the sun has come out and everything is bright and a bit exposed. Things have been looking so dead and grim. Now they are looking dead and grim and drowned.

Inside, here in the big room, the colour yellow is illuminated by the sun. There are daffodils and pears and bananas and chrysanthemums. Even the old yellow rotodex joins these yellow things in looking cheerful. Outside the window a small forsythia bush is in bloom. It reflects light and bright back into the room. This is more than just a promise of spring. I think this is spring, even though it is extremely soggy underfoot.

12 April—Two little girls visited yesterday. Their names were Ivy and Dora. They spent a long time collecting sticks for Em. They eagerly offered them to her one stick right after the other. She finally selected one long one and escaped to lie down in the shade for a chew of it. The girls piled the rest of the sticks outside her house. It now looks as though the dog is planning a huge bonfire.

14 April—I spent a few hours in Cahir this morning while Mike gave the car a check-up. It was cold. As I walked over the bridge, a woman wearing a heavy coat and mittens and a woolly hat nodded to me and shouted "Back to the caps again!"

There are not many errands that I need to do in Cahir. About half of all the shops are now empty anyway. Some have signs saying they are For Rent. I bought a newspaper and took a free copy of South Tipp Today. I read both papers while I drank a coffee and ate a fruit scone. Then I went to the SuperValu and did some grocery shopping. I did not want to buy too many things since I knew I had to carry everything up the hill to the garage. While there, I noticed another sign of the New Hard Times. The majority of products on the shelves were lined up along the front edge. Instead of an entire shelf being as full as it looked, it was very empty and dark behind a precarious single row. I went around and checked quite a few products to see if this was the norm. It was.

On the way back up the hill, I noticed a charity shop. Since I was still a bit early for picking up the car, I went in to look at the books. I found several things to read, but I saw no prices marked. I asked the girl at the counter how much the books were. She said "Oh please, just take them." She gave me a paper bag and told me to fill it up. After I chose six books, I went back to the counter and asked again if I could pay for them. She said no because she has too many books. Most of her customers are Foreign Nationals. They do not want to buy books in English. They are shopping for clothes and household things. She said if I have some things to bring in one day, she would appreciate it, but right now she is just desperate to get rid of the books.

19 April—Em is always on my left when I open the kitchen door to let her out. If I do it wrong and I am on the left and she is on the

right, she looks up at me and waits for me to move into the correct position before she goes outside.

20 April—Dessie has taken to driving his car way back into the field while he is working on his wood jobs. He turns on the radio in the car and opens all the doors so that he can hear it while he is working. He keeps the radio at top volume. It cannot be easy to hear it over the noise of power tools.

I went out there and asked him if I might have a few pallets, but he said No. He feels that he probably needs all the ones he has collected. He is cutting some of them up into small pieces for kindling. He says he will sell this kindling to a wholesaler. The other ones he is taking apart to provide fencing for his new house. There must be about eighty pallets piled up in the back. There are quite a few more in various states of deconstruction. He told me that they are no good for making my compost heap structure anyway because they will rot down too soon.

As I left, I took a good look at his Christmas tree decorations, which are still on a tree by the road. Most of the large bulbs have Budweiser written on them. They must have been some kind of pub decoration. Maybe he does not care about them, but I think he will want to reuse the lights at his new house, if he ever does actually move.

21 April—There are planes in the sky again. We cannot hear them but we can see their paths. The gap in the Icelandic ash is allowing things to get back to normal. I asked the postman what was happening to the post. We have only had a tiny bit of mail this week. We have received a few things from here in Ireland and a little bit from Britain. Nothing is arriving from any farther away. The postman said if this goes on much longer, they will start sending the post by boat from America and from mainland Europe. He said they are expecting a real deluge once things get going again. They have renamed Monday 'eBay Monday' in the sorting office since there are always so many packages to be delivered on a Monday. They are now preparing for the equivalent of a whole week of eBay Mondays.

24 April—We drove over the Knockmealdowns on the way home from Lismore. It was dark. I was a little nervous, as I always am when driving over these mountains at night. It is extremely dark up there at night and there are many places where it would be easy to plunge off the road and to fall a long distance.

As we came out of the wooded area into the higher parts of the mountains, we saw a red glow off to the left. Then we saw another red glow far off and up on the right. We thought this must be the burning of bracken which the hill farmers do yearly to keep the growth under control. It seemed strange for it to be being done at night, especially on such a dark night. There might have been a moon, but there was little light. Maybe it was cloudy. We kept coming across more and more burning areas, some quite close to the road. I had to close the window because the smoke was choking us. We drove up and around one bend and saw a big conflagration straight ahead of us. The fire was right down the banking and on the side of the road. The already narrow road was suddenly a single lane road because the fire had engulfed half of it. I slowed down but did not know what to do. I accelerated and rushed into and then out of the flames. We could feel the heat right through the closed windows and the sides of the car. I am still not sure if it was stupid or brave to drive right through the fire.

26 April—Em is much better. The only time we see a bit of the limp is when she gets up in the morning. A little early morning stiffness is not anything to worry about. I am still taking her for shorter rather than longer walks. The Mass Path is such a varied place for smells and exploring, I do not think she cares to go anywhere else anyway. Today as we walked along, Max joined us. He went for a swim in the stream with Em. Farther down the road, near Ken's house, Oscar joined us and they both came all the way down the boreen to our house. Em never dropped her stick and they never tried to take it from her. Oscar turned and went back home immediately upon arrival. Max stayed for a while, drank some water and then continued up the path back to his own house. Em did not seem interested either to have them with her, nor to have them leave again.

For many years she had Sydney hanging around, so I guess she just takes male companionship for granted. The difference with Syd was that he would never go home. We used to try all kinds of tricks to sneak away over Joe's fields when we thought Syd was not around. We did lots of things to stop him from following us on walks, but he always figured out everything. Sometimes he would rush to meet us from the opposite direction at great speed and with great joy. Whenever I sent him home, using a very stern voice, he would just go a little way up the road and lie down there. He was staying within earshot so that he would hear the car keys, the door, or any sound of food or cooking, walking or outdoor activity. Any of these sounds were enough to bring him dashing back into visible space. What he did not realize was that we could see the curve of his bottom just around the edge of the barn, so we knew he was there waiting and listening, even while he thought we could not possibly know that he was there.

In the year after his death, Simon made a little plaque using two old tractor windows fitted into an oval wooden frame. The letters etched on the glass are in black and white. Sydney himself was half greyhound and half something black and white. Three times the name Syd is written and then the date of his death and the words, very small: He Lived in the Fast Boreen. This is fixed to the stone wall of the barn, quite low down. The white curve of the frame shows just a little bit around the corner of the building. From the kitchen door, we can still look out and imagine that Syd is lying there, and that it is his hip that we are seeing. We can believe that he is just waiting for a single sound to bring himself rushing back into our lives.

27 April—I love to see Pigs Ears written on my shopping list. I buy five or six of them at a time and then cut them up into small pieces for Em. The garden shears are strong enough to cut them but it is hard work. They are tough and the edges of the ear and the gristly bits make the cutting difficult. I am getting better at choosing ones which might be easier to cut, but the nature of these smoked ears means that they will never be easy. As a result of the laborious nature of the job, sometimes Em receives an extremely tiny little sliver. I do not think she minds. It is just the ritual of getting a treat that matters.

1 May—There has been cold rain and hot sun intermittently all day. Each time the rain stops and the sun breaks through, there is another beautiful rainbow across the far field. Each rainbow is a distraction from whatever I am doing. I have lost count of the number of rainbows today.

2 May—Sometimes I spend so long listening to the Irish language radio that I forget that I do not understand it. I cannot tell anyone what I have heard, but I feel certain that I have understood it.

3 May—None of these roads are wide. Today Mickey the Boxer parked his car on the side of the road to go into a field and check on his cows. While he was getting things out of his car, a tractor came along pulling a big trailer. Then a car came from the opposite direction. The driver hooted his horn because he wanted to pass. Then he realized that he knew the farmer or the man in the tractor. He got out and greeted the two of them. Another tractor came along behind the first tractor. He stopped too. He had no choice. He got out and talked to everyone else who was gathered there. Em and I walked among and through them all. We greeted everyone as we went and continued on our way.

5 May—As we walked up the path in the sun, I saw an explosion of feathers on the ground which let me know that a pigeon had been eaten by a fox. There was nothing left but feathers. A few metres up the track I saw the wings of a bird spread out in a beautiful and perfect line. They were exactly in the position that they would be in if the bird was still there in the middle of them. I admired them for a few minutes and kept walking up the hill. Em did not come with me, nor did she answer my whistle a little later. When I went

back down to find her, she was just finishing her licking and chewing on the remnants of flesh that the fox had left on the ends of the wings. I was shocked that she had ruined the lovely birdless wing tableau. Sometimes I forget that she is a dog.

14 May—Dessie is gone. He has cleared everything and moved away. The elaborate fences that he made out of pallets and attached to the fence have been detached and taken away with him. He explained many times that he made them and attached them with a Special Method in order to be able to take them with him when he moved. He said he would leave them with the house only if the landlord paid him for them. He remembered to take the Christmas bulbs and the Christmas lights off the spruce tree. He took all his odd bits of equipment and everything that was laying around outside. The paving slabs made from casting several sizes of buckets are still in the ground. On the iron gate there remain a series of old fire screens which he wired on in the early days to keep the puppy from escaping. The place no longer looks like a garrison

in the Wild West. It just looks like a small empty white house in a field. I wonder if we will all revert to calling it the Murder Cottage, or will we speak of it as Dessie's House? Hardly anyone mentions it as Mary Corbett's Cottage any longer.

21 May—People from outside Ireland do not trust our address. They ask again and again for us to confirm its veracity. Six lines. One word per line. No numbers. It looks more like a shopping list than an address. Sometimes we make up a postal code just to make people from afar feel better.

22 May—Today we tried cooking rhubarb in the sun. We put the chopped up pieces in a plastic bag along with elderflower cordial, ginger and a bit of caster sugar. The bag was sealed and left out on the table in the very hot sun. We left it there while we sat gluing books into their covers in the cool barn. By the time the sun lost its heat, we still had a lot of books left to glue but the rhubarb was cooked.

28 May—Siobhán wants people to close the gate when they walk through to the backyard. She does not want her dog to escape out onto the road. She has been looking for a sign but she can't find one that doesn't use the word shut. She feels that it is rude to ask people to Shut the Gate or even Please Shut the Gate. She is looking for a sign to say exactly that but somehow she wants it to be more gentle.

29 May—The Cheese Lady was going to be away today, so we were invited to fill in for her at the Farmers' Market. We set up a small selection of our publications. Pat loaned us an awning, which was wonderful. It was like a little room. People could stand inside and under the awning while they looked at the books on our table. The people were out of the soft drizzle and the books were out of the soft drizzle. Most of the time it was not raining. We had a thoroughly pleasant time. It was both good to be on the other side of a table at the market and good for us to be able to show what we do to the people whose produce we buy every week. There was a lot of interest in the books as well as some lively conversation.

Normally Em loves the market and all the possibilities of dropped food. She loves the attention and the petting. I think she found four hours of scoping for things to nibble just too much hard work. She ended up sighing and sleeping heavily underneath our table.

30 May—The llama is back. I am not certain that he was ever really gone. He is just in a different field. This is not a field that I usually walk past. I will have to go out of my way if I want to continue our conversations about Peru. I do feel that he knows me now, or recognizes my voice. This is probably ridiculous. More likely he is just bored and the sound of any voice is a change from his lonely isolation in a field in Tipperary. Still, I am happy to see him again.

2 June—When I use the word Abroad, I am thinking of faraway places. I am thinking of a place usually overseas. I am thinking of a foreign place. Here the expression is used freely to describe someone being out and about. A farmer might be Abroad in the field. Or someone might be Abroad in the yard. They might just be Abroad, which suggests that they are somewhere other than at home, but definitely not overseas.

5 June—We always park down by the river when we go to the market. In the last few months, we have met the same man every Saturday. It does not matter if we arrive very early in the morning or if we arrive towards noon. He is always just arriving himself and he is getting out of his car as we walk up the hill. Each time he sees us, he admires and comments about Em and he wants to know how old she is. He then tells me about his own old dog. He tells me that his dog is sixteen years old and that his dog is going deaf. In the time that we have been having these conversations, his dog has gone completely deaf. His dog is a sheepdog. He can see that Em has sheepdog in her but that she is mixed with something else. Every Saturday I tell him that we do not know who her father was. Every Saturday I tell him that we got her from the daughter of Mr. Fitzgerald, the local man who sold us our washing machine. He knows Mr. Fitzgerald and tells me this each time. He always tells me that Em reminds him of the Dulux dog on television. It is just that that dog is cute and black and white, and Em is cute and black and white too. They are not the same kind of dog at all. We have the same conversation every week. The only change is in the health of his own dog. Otherwise the entire conversation is exactly as it was the week before. I have taken to calling this man the Dulux Man. Simon has taken to walking quickly up the hill and away as soon as the conversation begins.

7 June—Michael O'Connor is dead. He has been dead for three months now, maybe four. I commented to Tommie about the small

car that is parked in Michael's yard. For as long as I have lived here, Michael has never had a car. He had a bicycle, but not a car. In the last few years, he never even went out on his bicycle. He stayed inside his gate and in his yard and he just walked about a little bit. Tommie told me that the car is there as a decoy. He explained that it is there so that no one will know that the house is empty. He told me that this was the function of a decoy. He told me this as though I were stupid.

21 June—Over the last few days, there has been a lot of noise from up at Maisie's old house. The old house has been gone for a year now and a new house has been built, but we still speak of the place as Maisie's. A digger has been working long hours to move all of the house rubble. It was all in a big pile out back by the sheds, and the digger has been sorting it. I noted  the progress every time Em and I passed on foot. We could hear the working machinery all the way down here if the wind was coming from the right direction.

This morning we saw that there are now twelve small mountains of rubble down near Em's swimming place. Twelve Mountains and Two Very large Cubes of Concrete. The mountains are made up of the knocked down house materials. There are very few stones among the rubble. The large stones are still up the hill in the big pile by the sheds. This pile is a good distance from the new house. It took the digger several days to carefully sift, sort and separate the stones from the rubble. It has all been transported quite a distance down through the fields to get to where it is now.

Em and I walked between the mountains. They are all the same size and they are all equally spaced. Each mountain is taller than me. It is a tidy installation in an odd location. By road, all of this detritus is a kilometer and a half from the house it once was. I guess the spot was chosen because it is the farthest point in the fields and therefore the least useful for growing things and for moving farm machinery in and around.

24 June—The long bench outside of my workroom was a good idea. When we made it, we planned it for sitting and admiring the view from a pleasing vantage point. The deep overhang of the eaves

means the bench is protected from most rain. It spans the length of the front of the building between the two doors. It is five and a half metres long but a little bit higher than I would like. When I sit on it, my feet dangle off the ground. It ended up a bit high because when the blacksmith came with the metal brackets he had made, he had to put them into the wall in a place where the wall would take them. There was a bit of lumpiness down near the bottom, so

the bench got raised higher off the ground. The smooth wooden boards make a wide and comfortable surface, but in spite of the generosity of the width, the bench seems to be used for everything except sitting.

Underneath, it has become one of our firewood storage places. It is a good and protected spot and what is stored there now is dry and will be ready for next winter. I use the bench as a kind of table, an extension of my workroom. At the moment, I have lined up a fine selection of the rusted objects I've found and collected. It looks as if I might be opening a little shop.

We spent a lot of time as children making shops to sell groceries. We emptied my mother's cupboards of cans and containers. We made labels for empty boxes and assorted packages to further fill our shelves. I do not remember ever getting to the point where we sold anything to anyone. The whole activity was about setting up the shop. My line-up of rusty things is for no purpose. It is just good to see them all together and to admire them as I walk past. Sometimes I bring things inside to make drawings of them.

25 June—John the Post always has an apple in his van. Sometimes when I see him, he is eating it and sometimes it is waiting to be eaten. He leaves it sitting in the box with the letters he has not yet delivered. I am wondering if he leaves his house each day with a large supply of apples for the morning delivery route, or if he just takes the one.

30 June—For the first time in eighteen months we took Em to the sea. She went mad and ran and ran and ran in and out of the water. Her eyes were those of a deranged animal. She was so wet and covered with sand and seaweed and barking hysterically that

she frightened several small children. By the time we got home, she could barely walk. I was worried. We had let her overdo the running. Her exhaustion was complete, but after a bit of rest, there was no sign of the old limp returning.

Hill farmers from the Comeragh Mountains used to take their sheepdogs down to the sea every year to sooth or maybe to toughen their feet in the salt water. I like the idea of a truckload of sheepdogs going for their yearly outing to the seaside.

2 July—The Twelve Mountains of Maisie have been flattened. The area is now a hard surface with the bits of recognizable rubble all evened out. There are visible chunks of a wall that was once painted green. It was certainly an inside wall. It must have made for a very dark room. There are not too many other colours visible. Everything else is cement grey or brown or a dirty white, but somehow the overall colour feels light. The new flat area looks more like an interior space than the dark ground of out-of-doors.

The two big cubes of concrete have been pushed off to the side by the trees of Cooney's wood. They were not crushed. They look like large dice.

5 July—There was a young woman in a clothes shop in town. She was overweight, but she insisted on trying on a very tiny dress. She was going to a party and wanted to look terrific. She spoke in a loud excited voice so that everyone in the shop knew all about the party. It was quiet after she disappeared into the dressing room but before long we all heard a shriek. She squealed, "I can't go out like this! I look like a cat in a sock!"

6 July—I meet Michael almost every other morning now. Simon and I take turns walking Em up the boreen and around. She is happiest with this regular short walk and a swim. The one of us not going with Em is free to go the longer route around the fields and up Flemingstown way. Most days when I walk the long way I meet Michael. We seem to be on the same time clock. He is on his way to help Joe with the cows. Some days he is in the tractor and some days he is in his car. If he turns off the engine, I know that we are going to have a long chat. Sometimes another vehicle comes and that puts an end to the conversation. Usually we spend 15 or 20 minutes before continuing in our opposite directions.

Today the subject came up of people having to give up driving when they get too old to be safe on the road. He called it Taking the

Father Out of the Car. We spoke of a local man who is now eighty-six. He no longer drives at night and he does not drive very far from his home. He drives extremely slowly, which annoys other drivers. We are thinking that he might have to give up driving soon. We spoke of various other people who have had to give up driving and we spoke of the sense of no longer being in control of one's own life and movements. We spoke about the loss of independence. Michael said sadly that it was a terrible decision to have to make for someone else.

9 July—A young farmer from down the road got married today. He and his new wife drove off to their reception in a tractor. It was not his own tractor but a vintage one belonging to a friend. Or this is what we were told. We went into Nugent's for a drink and, as we sat there talking, the room filled up with young men and women. The smell of aftershave and perfume was strong. There was a lot of hair gel and everyone was wearing their fancy clothes, as opposed to the usual Friday night after work gear. Ironed shirts and pressed jeans, heels and glittery dresses. Everyone was drinking and waiting. They were all pretty early, but the waiting was part of the ritual. Eventually the McCarra's bus would come to collect everyone and take them into town for The Afters.

The Afters is what happens After the church wedding ceremony and After the dinner and After the speeches. The Afters is the party that celebrates the marriage. Everyone is invited to The Afters. Most times it is in a large venue like a hotel, but sometimes it is in a big tent set up for the purpose. There will be a band and dancing and a pay bar. It will go on until the early hours. It will go on until the bus comes to take everyone home. We left before the bus arrived, so I do not know how much longer they all spent gathering and drinking and readying themselves. I think some of them were going to be ready to collapse before they even got to The Afters.

11 July—What I call the Yellow Pages are called the Golden Pages here. The telephone book is made of the same thin newsprint sort of paper and the shade of yellow is the same as it is in other places, but here the pages are called golden. It makes them sound special.

17 July—The Dulux Man was very sad to tell me that his dog is now going blind as well as being deaf. He is extremely depressed about this. Every year he and his dog have entered the dog show at the Cahir Fair. Every single year that he has entered, he and his dog

have won three prizes. This year he felt he could not enter The Tree Run. The Tree Run is when the owner tells his dog to run to the tree and back and the dog does exactly that. His dog can no longer hear the command nor see the tree. The Dulux Man said the dog was Not Able For It. I do not know what the other categories were, but he was most disappointed about The Tree Run.

21 July—When I am out walking in the morning, I often meet John the Post. Sometimes he just waves, and sometimes he stops to chat. If he has not been to our house yet, he gives me the mail. If there is a small packet or parcel, he asks me if I can manage to carry the parcel or will it ruin my walk? I always say it is okay because he never gives me anything that is too large to carry. Today I took a few things from him and then he started to drive down the hill. He did not accelerate. He just rolled along in his van and I walked along beside him and we continued our conversation through his open window. We moved along like this for a good distance until another car came up behind him and he had to move along. We were taking up the whole road.

22 July—Damp and grey. Wet and cool. It does not feel the way I would like July to feel. Em is happy because she does not like warm mornings. She prefers this damp coolness. She is an Irish dog. As we walked, I stopped again at the flattened area of what was once Maisie's Mountains well after it was Maisie's House. The area of rubble had been so firmly evened out that I felt certain that it would be years before anything grew there. Last week as I walked around on the hard surface, I saw that small bits of grass and weeds were already growing through the rubble. I began to pick up the pieces of Maisie's green painted wall. These pieces are just clumps of concrete with a skim of plaster on the flat surface. The dark green was painted over an earlier shade of green. The first green looks much brighter than the second green. I gathered up a number of the pieces and placed them in a group, green side up, in the middle of the flattened rubble. Today I returned to this job and doubled my area of green pieces. Most of the bits are small. The largest piece I have found so far is no more than eight inches across.

All the time I was wandering about and collecting the pieces of green, Em was waiting for me down in the stream. She did not bark. She just waited. She stood in the water quietly looking up at the place from which I throw the daily stick. Every once in a while I called out to her and I said that I would be there soon. She could have come out of the water at any time and joined me on the rubble surface, but she has had no interest in that place since the mountains were flattened. I am becoming obsessed with this area. I wonder if I can collect the whole green room. I wonder if I can collect the whole green room and lay it all out on the rubble before the surface is overtaken by vegetation.

26 July—I returned my library books today. I placed the books on

the counter and apologized because the books were late. I asked how much I owed for them. The librarian said I owed nothing at all. I said, "They are four days late, I must owe something." She said "No, you're grand. There is a one-week grace period. You're grand." All these years, I have been rushing to return my books promptly after the three-week loan period, and all these years, everyone else has known that the date stamped in the front of the book doesn't really mean a thing.

28 July—I have done a few more days of collecting for the Green Room. That is how I think of the pieces of green from the rubble of Maisie's house. It is getting harder and harder to find the pieces of green. I fear that without a better tool, I will soon be finished with the collection process. I use whatever stick I have with me. It is usually the same stick which Em is waiting to have thrown into the water. I can see a few large and thick pieces stuck firmly between other rocks and rubble. I cannot get them out by hand or with a stick. I need a shovel or a spade or a crowbar if I am going to get at these pieces.

Most of the greens which I now retrieve are no bigger than a coin. In the beginning, I could double the area size of the green pieces each time I stopped at the site. Now, with such tiny fragments, and even these becoming harder to find, I am lucky to add a narrow strip of colour down one side of my area. The dream of laying out the whole room has changed. Now I hope to maybe get enough pieces to equivalence one wall.

2 August—I was back in the Green Room this morning. I am discouraged with my lack of progress. I do not want to begin a major job of removal. I do not want to dig up all the flattened down rubble. I just enjoy the collecting.

I was eager to spread out the green surface before the new vegetation took over. Now I have to acknowledge that the vegetation is winning. Everything grows so fast here. One year we had weeds growing up out of the damp floor mat inside the van. Compared to that, this arrival of weeds in an inhospitable area of old concrete and plaster and stone is not much of a challenge.

Maybe this Green Room I have in my head was never a room, but only a Green Wall. Maybe it was a section of a wall and not even a whole wall. Maybe my collection of the greens is not so far off the original size of that area which Maisie painted green. I am trying to reassure myself, but it is not working. I shall try to find out if anyone remembers the colour green inside her house. If I had not been so squeamish about the cat smells I might have seen the inside of her kitchen. I would have seen the green wall or the green room and I would know what the area is that I am trying to replicate.

9 August—As I walked up past Michael O'Connor's house, I saw his brother Johnnie loading up a trailer outside the door. I stopped to speak since I had not seen him, even to offer my condolences, since Michael died last winter. Johnnie knew that Michael called me American Lady, so he greeted me like that himself today. He told me he was there to clear out a few more things while he waited for the auctioneer. The house was already very empty. Johnnie told me how he and his wife had painted and fixed up the place seventeen years ago for Michael when he moved over from England. He told me that he and Michael had been two of nine children. He spoke of various deaths and of the order of the siblings and about who was left. On the wall near the door, there was a photograph of a much younger Michael in a group of people. Johnnie told me a few stories about Michael over the years. He said that Michael had never got his driving license but that he had taken lessons in England. He once got to the point of taking his test. He drove around for a while doing whatever the examiner asked him to do. When they passed a pub that Michael knew well, he pulled up to the curb and said "We'll have a drink here now, will we?"

10 August—An old man from the Nire came into the bar. As soon as he arrived, Rose was busy trying to organize a lift home for him.

Someone had dropped him off and she knew he would never leave unless she got him going on his way. She was eager for him not to stay. He had not even finished his pint of cider when she had a lift waiting. He quickly purchased a Naggin of whiskey to take with him. This was a new word for me. A Naggin is a quarter bottle, usually of whiskey but it might be brandy. The old man slipped the Naggin into the voluminous pockets of his baggy trousers. It was just the right size to fit into the pockets of that kind of trousers. I had not really felt like stopping in for a drink at Rose's, but the word Naggin makes me glad I did.

12 August—We spoke to a dentist who arrived in a bright red sports car. It was a two-seater with a convertible soft top. In the course of conversation, he told us that he did not like to drive fast. He said that the only reason he had a sports car was that he did not like to have empty seats behind him when he drove.

15 August—I am giving up on the Green Room. The weeds are winning. This morning I spent more time pulling out weeds than I did finding more pieces of green painted plaster. Each time I have stopped there this week, I have found fewer and fewer fragments. I have resisted bringing along a tool to make the work easier. The area of pieces which I have laid down looks very fine. The pieces hidden away in the rubble will remain hidden and this little area will remain my private memory of Maisie. When things die down in the winter, it might reappear. No one but myself will stop to look at it, but I will know it is there.

1 September—When a registered letter comes, the postman does not ask us to sign for it. Instead, he just signs for it himself and drops it into our plastic post box. Sometimes he asks us a few days later if we got that registered letter which he put into the box. Most times he never mentions it.

2 September—I cannot stop thinking about the Green Room. I thought I should stop and clear the weeds from directly around the green shards and make a photograph of them being overtaken by vegetation. I was not sure that I could get the camera directly over the area to get a straight down shot with no parallax. Since there is nothing to stand on and since I am short, I thought I would just do the best I could. I thought a lot about how to do this as I walked down the track with Em.

When we reached the site, I was shocked to see the whole surface covered with huge leafy branches. Woodcutters were in Cooney's wood thinning out trees. The sound of chainsaws was not too loud because they were deep into the forest. Dragging timber all the way out to be piled on the rubble surface seemed crazy, but that looks like exactly what they are doing. I do not think I will ever see Maisie's Green Room again.

9 September—We have printed a book in China. The whole shipment is traveling by ship to Rotterdam. The ship is called the Mol Maxim. From Rotterdam, the books will be put onto another ship heading for Dublin. After they clear customs, they will travel by road to Kilkenny and then on to us here. This journey will take some weeks. With the world and everything in it moving so quickly, I find it reassuring to have this element of time involved in the production of a book. Of course, FedEx or some courier could do it faster, but with FedEx, we would not know the name of the ship doing the carrying.

11 September—This morning's weather forecast promised a day that would be light and breezy, sunny with rainy spells which might be squally and sometimes heavy. This forecast covers just about every eventuality, except snow.

12 September—I lifted all my potato crop because there seem to be some little holes in many of the potatoes. I do not think worms or bugs are still inside but I think the potatoes will be better out of the ground. Usually we just leave them in the soil and dig them as we want to eat them. I dried them off on the outside table for the day and have now put them in a big barrel. This is an experiment and I hope it works. The onions are now all tied in groups of four or five and are hanging in a row in the shed. There are eighteen bunches. They are so beautiful that I have been walking into the shed all day just to admire them again and again. The smell is wonderful. It fills the whole shed.

14 September—There are thousands of butterflies in the garden. I have never seen so many butterflies in one place. I have heard of this kind of swarming but I have never seen it before, and I have certainly not seen it here. These are all the same kind of butterflies. I'm told that they are Red Admirals. They are on flowers and bushes

and even on the grass. Every day they appear with the sunshine and then they disappear by sundown. Every day I think it will be the last day for this magic. Em was sleeping in the sun yesterday with masses of the butterflies all around and upon her. She looked like a celebration.

 16 September—Irishtown is the part of Clonmel that is outside the West Gate. When the English were in control here, the Irish could work in the town during the day but they had to go outside at night. Only the English slept safely inside the fortified walls and gates. The houses and shops in the area outside the gate are still spoken of as being in Irishtown. The street does not have a name. The street itself is called Irishtown.

There is a house a few blocks down from the gate with a big front window. I assume this house used to be a shop and that is why there is a large window. For several years there has been a dog who sat in the window. He sat in the window which was once probably for displaying wares. A curtain behind the dog provided privacy for the people in the house. He watched people pass on the street. Sometimes he barked, sometimes he slept and sometimes he would not be there at all, so he was probably hanging around in another part of the house or maybe he was out for a walk. The dog was small and fat and old. He was some sort of mixed breed, and brown in colour. I cannot even begin to describe what he was, but he was not attractive. He was very much a part of the walk up that side of the street in Irishtown. If I saw him or if I did not see him was not important. What was important was that I always looked to see if he was there or not.

Today I walked past the house and there was a small wooden box on the windowsill. It is the length of a shoe box but it is more narrow than a shoebox. The box is nicely sanded and finished with some matte varnish and there is a little metal plaque on the top with the name ROBBIE engraved on it. The box is not big enough to actually contain the dog, so I assume that it is holding Robbie's ashes.

18 September—There is a lot of crossing of oneself as people pass churches here. I see people doing it while they drive. They do it when they walk. Today I saw a man crossing himself while he was driving and talking into a mobile phone at the same time.

20 September—We have a local phone book which is years out of date now. This book was put together by a local group as a fundraiser. All telephone numbers have had a 61 added to them and now everyone has mobiles so it is hard to know where to begin in re-listing a lot of these numbers and many of the local addresses. I cannot just throw away the old book but it is hard to use it. People do not move house very much but the numbers are all different. The book is tattered and its blue cover is no longer attached.

I heard a woman in a shop complaining that her address book was all filled up on the M and the O pages. She said that she had never yet found an address book to accommodate those letters properly for the Irish. That is another problem to consider.

29 September—The sky is heavy and grey and dark. There is a strange quality of light through the darkness which makes the grass glow. This shade of green is one that I have only ever seen here. It is luminous in its brightness. The luminosity is not beautiful. It is somehow creepy and garish. If it were painted in a picture, it would look wrong. If it were photographed, it would look wrong. Maybe that is why it looks so wrong now as I look across the fields. It is an impossible colour.

2 October—The Toothpaste House just up from Booding Bridge has been painted. It is now white. The minty blue-green colour which glowed from across the valley is gone. Of course toothpaste comes in white but we would never name a white house The Toothpaste House. This house is low and not too long. From here, its former colour sat on the hillside just like a line of toothpaste on a toothbrush. Now that it is white, it is just another house.

7 October—I detoured through the car park of the old Crazy Prices store in Clonmel. As I walked, I saw a truck with a big white sign with red letters advertising CASH FOR CLOTHES. I thought about this as I did my errands, so when I returned I went over to the truck to see what it was about. How is money being made with Cash for Clothes? It was yet another sign of the New Austerity and Hard Times, but I could not figure out how it worked. A man was sitting on a plastic chair inside the truck, drinking a cup of coffee. There were big black plastic sacks piled up behind him. They looked as if they were stuffed full of clothing. I asked if he was really paying for old clothes. He said yes. I asked him how he paid. I was imagining something like a set price per garment: like five euro for a coat. He

said he paid fifty cent a kilo. I said "But you don't have a scales here. How do you know how much things weigh?" He held out his hand, palm open and up, and said, "This is my scales."

22 October—I was at the supermarket today and went into the sheltered unit to return my trolley and to get my euro coin refunded. Between myself and the trolleys a small elderly man was sheltering from the wind while having a pee. He waved to me with his free hand and said, "No worry! I'd be nearly done!"

31 October—Tom Browne is in hospital. He has cancer and is not doing well with this on top of his many strokes. His wife rang to see if we had a bottle of Guinness that she could take to him. The hospital had phoned her and asked her to bring in a bottle in the hope of stimulating his appetite. I was quite surprised by this as a request from a hospital but apparently it is not an unusual procedure when a patient is not eating. I gather that it was more normal in the past, but that it is still a useful method when someone remembers to try it. Unfortunately, it is not possible to buy a bottle of Guinness anywhere on a Sunday morning, so I do not know if she found a bottle, or if it worked to stimulate his appetite.

4 November—Yesterday our electricity went off at about four o'clock in the afternoon. I walked up to see if the farm had lost its power too. It had. They have a generator in the event of a power loss but for some reason it was not wired up. I talked to the electricity men who arrived looking for a break in the cables. By the time I walked back home, it was dark. I tried to get on with some things but it is amazing how much we expect everything to function as usual and without electricity it just doesn't. Water does not even come out of the taps if the electric pump doesn't work to bring it from the well. We gave up doing anything and went down to the village to see if the lights were off there.

On the way we checked up on a few older neighbours to make sure they had candles and torches. The lights were off everywhere and as we looked across the hills, we could see that see that everywhere was very, very dark. The only lights we saw were the flashing yellow lights from the repair trucks in different distant locations.

We went into Rose's where a few people were sitting at the bar drinking things that came in bottles because the pressure pumps for draught drinks were not working. There were a few candles lit on the bar and there was quiet conversation. A few songs were sung, again very quietly. One man had driven down from way up the mountain. He knew that if it was just his own house without power, he would have to wait for many days to get it repaired, but if the electricity was down everywhere, it would be repaired quickly. He just had to come down to find out. At half eight or so, the lights came back on and so did the television. A football match was on and together with that noise, the fluorescent lights turned the bar into a completely different place. We came home and ate dinner by candlelight just to hold on to the quiet.

6 November—I have just found out that the Gloomy Donkey is named Morris or Maurice. Since this is a French breed of donkey, I think it's probably Maurice. I never thought of him as having a name. While I have been worrying about this Gloomy Donkey being lonely, I am now told that he has taken to biting people. The reason he is alone in the meadow is because he killed his baby and began attacking his wife. I have less reason than ever to stop and talk with this creature, but I am curious to know why he is so mean.

16 November—The Large Apple Path is more slippery than ever. It smells like a cider press as I struggle along it. In contrast, the Crab Apple Path is not breaking down at all. That section is still wildly precarious for walking and for balance. The colours are good. The crab apples themselves are bright yellowy green and they are scattered among leaves which are brown, yellow and gold. The leaves are all small and they pile upon each other delicately. On top of the leaves are hundreds of bright red berries. In among all this, there are stones covered with bright green moss. The moss is so bright, it is nearly fluorescent.

18 November—With all the trouble that this country and this government are in, I was surprised to get my free stamp at the post office today. The yearly Christmas gift of one free stamp when one buys a book of 55 cent inland stamps has not come under the attack of the new budget, or not yet anyway. At 13 euro 75, 26 stamps for the price of 25 feels like a real treat.

19 November—We stopped in at the pub. Rose had been waiting to give me fifty-eight euro. She had been saving it in a glass until I next came in. I had won the little lottery which the pub does every week. It is predicated on the bonus number for the big national lottery. We do not usually buy chances on this but someone had convinced us to participate because they were lacking enough participants that week. If they did not get enough numbers, it would be a very small prize for anyone to win. The chart with the numbers is ruled out on a piece of cardboard. The cardboard is cut from the inside of a cereal box. It has to be drawn on cardboard rather than paper because it gets passed around a lot and some people spend a long time deciding which number they will choose. A piece of paper would get too ratty over the course of a week. A name is written in the little box beside the chosen number. My winning number was 2.

An old man was sitting at the bar. I had never seen him there before. He introduced himself as Peter. He had enormous sticking out ears. Peter was down for the weekend to visit his cousin. He had ridden on the bus from Carlow and she had collected him in Clonmel. When the bells for the Angelus began to ring on the television, he took off his flat cap and put it tightly under his armpit. He said quietly, "Now it is time to pray." He closed his eyes tight and his lips moved silently throughout the bell tolling. When the bells stopped, he stopped, and put his cap back on his head. He continued to recite things about himself. One thing was that he 'took himself off the road' directly after he had a run-in with a tractor. That was some years ago. He no longer drives but he enjoys

taxis and loves sitting high up in the bus. He loves having a bus pass for free travel. It was good to hear him ramble on. There are not many of these old men to bump into these days. They are either afraid of the drink-driving laws or they are without the money needed to come out for a pint.

This man was not at all interested in my lottery win. In fact, he was not interested in me at all. He was interested to do all the talking himself.

20 November—Everything around here is done at the last minute. On Thursday, I got a message asking me to gather up books to

take to a fundraising sale. All books at the sale would be priced at two euro. I thought it would be a good idea to sort out some things to take along for this good cause. Then I saw that the things donated must be delivered by the next morning, a Friday, in order to be ready for the sale on Saturday. Why couldn't I be given more notice? With proper notice, my gathering together of stuff could be considered and efficient. When announcements are sent out for exhibitions, the theory is to do it at the last minute because, if it is announced too far in advance, everyone will forget about it and then they won't attend. If no one can plan for anything, that means everyone is always dropping things for something more immediate.

Death is always demanding. If someone dies today, there will be a wake tomorrow and the funeral will be the next day. Death commands an immediacy that does not allow for any questions.

21 November—We heard the loud sound of a flock of geese passing in the sky. Looking up, we expected to see them moving in formation, but we saw nothing. It took a few minutes to recognize that the sound was not geese at all but a cow bellowing in the field above.

27 November—Today was Tom Browne's funeral. It took place at the church in Fourmilewater. I had never been inside that church. It is a large building and looks larger because of the way it sits on a slope leading down into the graveyard. We sat next to a radiator because the day was bitterly cold. The radiator was warm, but not hot. The heat did not radiate much.

The inside of the church was painted pale yellow, except for the end wall behind the priest, which was painted pale green. Along the walls were light fixtures comprised of two fluorescent tubes inside long rectangular plastic covering devices, not unlike what would be found on the ceiling of an office or a shop. These lighting units were hung vertically, placed between stained-glass windows and at intervals up around behind the altar. Each unit started about eight or nine feet from the floor. I had a lot of time to look around because I do not participate in any of the kneeling, prayer repetition and responses which keep everyone else busy.

As usual at these Catholic funerals, there was no singing and, indeed, no music of any sort. At one point, the two altar girls, wearing heavy jackets on top of their robes, rang some bells in response to something the priest said. Through one very lightly coloured window, we all kept an eye on the snow which was falling faster and thicker all through the service. The priest, who was wearing a winter coat too, placed various tools on Tom's coffin: a plasterer's float, a trowel, a dusting brush and something else. Then he said he would cut the prayers short so that we could get Tom buried before the snow got worse. Once outdoors, the bitter wind and driving snow forced everything to be shortened again. People jumped into their cars and many just raced home to beat the storm.

We went along to The Hidden Inn, where there were fried chicken legs and little sausages and hundreds of small triangular sandwiches on white bread all waiting to be eaten. Copious quantities of hot tea were drunk. I had three cups in quick succession. Everyone was frozen to the bone. After the tea, people moved on to pints of Guinness or glasses of whiskey or brandy and quiet toasts. There were many older men there who had worked with Tom over the years. His strength, his gracefulness and his skill at his trade were all discussed. One man claimed that Tom Browne could draw out a dolphin in plaster without even thinking about it. Discussion returned again and again at how funny it was that the tools on the coffin were all brand new. Everyone knew that Tom had never owned new tools. He consistently fixed, repaired and improvised with what he had and with what he found around a building site.

We did not stay long. I wonder if many people did. There was none of the music or boisterousness of some other funerals. Tom's absence over the recent years had not meant that he was forgotten, just that his non-presence was already a norm. The threat of the snow and the cold was not much incentive for people to linger.

2 December—Simon drove down to the village this morning. He was nervous about driving over the humpbacked bridge but it had been gritted and felt safe. When he left the bridge and got onto the straight, flat stretch of road, the car slid out of control and he smashed into the stone wall. Then the car kept sliding around and he smashed into the same wall with the opposite end of the car. Both ends are a mess but the motor still works. He was able to drive home but was shaken by it all. Since the entire country is broke, it is not a surprise that the county council has no money to spend on spreading sand and salt on the roads. In many ways, this unexpected early winter weather is a great distraction from the discussions of the desperate economic situation, but in other ways it just points out the inefficiency and the lack of planning that created the mess in the first place.

5 December—Rushing out to the sauna through the crunchy snow in a dressing gown and little rubber clogs was terrible tonight. My shoulders were hunched as high as was possible up around my ears. I was wishing that I had worn a wool hat, a scarf and a coat and socks. I was wishing that I was fully dressed. As I entered the sauna, the heat took my breath away. Very quickly, the short chilly journey was forgotten. The outdoor tap was frozen, so there was no chance of a cold shower. I did love strolling back across the dark yard, with my torch, crunching again, but no longer feeling the cold.

6 December—Last night, I heard on the radio that rats are suffering in this cold. They are desperate to get inside. They want to enter houses, barns, rubbish bins, anywhere at all to find food and warmth. The programme made the threat feel so real, I panicked. Before going to bed, I put the plug into the bathtub. Just in case.

7 December—Em and I walked our usual walk around today. As we went past the house where Susie and Shep live, I saw that the gates were wide open. Most times, this suggests that the two dogs are hanging well back and peering at the road from behind some of the trees. There are dozens and dozens of trees there. The yard is a densely planted forest. The owner intends to grow all his own fuel eventually. His plan is a constantly thinned forest, making way for more planting at the same time as some larger trees continue to grow and grow.

The dogs have only ever been barking and brave when they are safe behind the gate. Today was the exception. They rushed out of the yard and attacked Em. She was on her back in seconds and was struggling hard to fight off the two young dogs. She is old and they are young and there were two of them, so they were much bolder. Max, who was walking with us, and who was the biggest dog by far, barked and barked and jumped up and down. He did not help with the attack nor did he try to see off the attackers. He just barked. I shouted and then I whacked the dog nearest to me. I kept shouting and ordering them home and eventually they rushed back into the trees. Em ran down the road with Max rushing behind her. He was gleeful and she was shaking.

When we got home, I found only one small bit of torn flesh on Em, so the battle was not too bad. I think I am more upset than she is. We have never had a fight with another dog in all the years of walking we have done around here.

9 December—Talking to other neighbours, I have found out more about Susie and Shep. I had thought that they were the gentlest and most cowardly pair of sheepdogs ever. They are, in fact, a vicious duo. They build up a grudge against a passing dog and then attack whenever possible. Coco is one of their targets. Now I guess Em is too. Max is too big to attack and, anyway, they have known him since they were puppies. I am astounded at how completely I could misunderstand their characters.

I have the same feeling about Maurice. All the time I thought of him as yet another Gloomy Donkey. Now I think of him as malevolent. When I pass his meadow, I call out "Hello Maurice, you Beast!" Sometimes he acknowledges my greeting and sometimes he does not.

10 December—We drove the little car over to Mike today. We drove slowly. The car got hot and overheated. It is all much worse than we thought. It took Mike forty minutes just to get the bonnet open. The radiator is destroyed as are a lot of other parts of the motor. It has been declared dead. It is not worth spending money to repair it. The country is full of second-hand cars. Everyone is selling and no one is buying. In this case, repairing is not an option. Mike drove us home in his Jeep. Once here, he towed out the big Volvo, which has been paralyzed in position by the ice for ten days. The whole exhaust system had been ripped off too. He fixed that and now we'll leave it parked up at the farm until this ice melts or breaks up. Most of the roads around are clear now but our own ice is not giving up.

14 December—A group of thirty-five little boys in red and white Santa Claus hats played their instruments for passing shoppers in the Market Place. In three positions near to the band were pairs of boys also wearing the red and white hats. One boy held a huge plastic margarine bucket with a slot cut in the top. He shook the

bucket so that we passersby could hear the sound of the coins inside it. He shook the bucket to encourage us to put money into the bucket. The other boy waved a tambourine at people and hit it against his hand or against the other boy at intervals.

Each pair of boys were a bit shy about approaching people. They stepped back a few steps when anyone came to put money in their bucket. I guess they were all nine or ten years old. The band's version of O Tannenbaum was the worst I have ever heard. The teacher kept conducting and the boys played with enthusiasm, but the music got no better.

16 December—We went to fetch the new car at Mike's. He has had it at his garage since Tuesday. On Tuesday, he and Simon went together to Tipperary town and met a man in the supermarket car park. The man was on his lunch hour. They looked at the car and discussed it. They made test drives and then Simon bought the car. The car is not new. It is a 1995 Volvo but, compared to our 1988 version, it is New. This one only has 170,000 miles on the clock. Ours had close to 400,000. These cars do go and go. It was extremely cheap because no one wants to bother with a car this old. Even though it was cheap, Simon talked the price down a little bit. This was all part of the accepted behaviour. After he paid the man the agreed price, the man took 50 euro out of his pocket and gave it back to Simon For Luck. This is also agreed behaviour.

Today, Mike demonstrated all the details and differences of this new model. The former owner had typed up little labels. These labels were stuck down on various parts of the immaculately clean engine. Each label identified when a new part had been installed and was followed by a number like 140K. This was his code to say, for example, that a new fan belt had been installed at 140,000 miles. I should make a list of all these labels before life down this muddy old track changes all the clean labels and the clean engine forever.

20 December—While standing in the library waiting to have my books checked out, I listened to the librarian talking with the woman in front of me. The woman was talking about the problem of reading heavy books in bed. She said that finally she had given up on large and cumbersome books in bed. Only smaller books were now read in her bed. The woman asked the librarian if she had the same problem. The librarian said that when she went to bed, she turned off the light and went to sleep. The librarian said she never read anything in bed. The woman and I looked at each other. We

were not quite speechless, but we both had looks of surprise on our faces. The woman asked me if I read in bed. I said, "Indeed, I do read in bed. Bed is my very favourite place for reading."

The librarian said that she has a small table in one corner of her kitchen. She has a good lamp on the table and her ashtray as she likes to sit and smoke cigarettes and read. She said that she likes to smoke almost every minute that she is reading. She said, "Sometimes I do not know if I read while I smoke or if I smoke while I read."

I have noticed that sometimes my library books smell like cigarette smoke. It is usually things like thrillers and mysteries that have this strong odour. I am never very happy to have this smell in my bed with me. Often I can still smell it even when the book is closed and the light switched off. I have considered having a good sniff of my chosen books before I leave the library but I always forget to do it. Now when I next get into bed with a smoky book, I shall just assume that it was recently read by the librarian herself. I shall picture her sitting at her little table smoking while she reads for hours on end.

24 December—The Council came and filled holes in the road yesterday. I have been trying to get them to come and do this since last winter. It is still bumpy but compared to two days ago, it is wonderful. This morning, we walked the mile and a half to a neighbour's house to take showers. With clean clothes and towels in our backpacks, we admired the hole filling as we walked up the boreen and then we admired it all again as we walked back down a few hours later.

The cold is not letting up. Our lives seem to be about nothing but survival and staying warm. Now the out pipes have been frozen for a few days too. Everywhere we have water in buckets and containers. There are ladles and small and large pitchers. We have bottles of bought water and water bottles filled with tap water from other taps than our own. There are different waters for different jobs. Everything, even washing a few dishes, is a complicated job. The water must be decanted into a kettle or a pot and heated on the stove. Then it is poured into a small dishpan and a bit more is poured into another small dishpan. Things are washed and rinsed and then the water must be thrown outside. It is terrible to go outside with wet hands to empty the water. It is best to dry one's hands and put on mittens before doing even this very quick job.

We are trying to use as few dishes as possible. Two water glasses

sit on the big table. There is one for each of us.
We have used these same two water glasses
all week. We will continue to use them. I keep
thinking of the farmers all over the country who
are having a terrible time getting water to their
animals. Their tasks are enormous compared
to our small issues. In the middle of our own
situation, I cannot really imagine their problems.
Selfishly, I can think only about the most
immediate things, and right now everything is
an immediate thing.

28 December—Yesterday morning the waste
pipes thawed and this morning we have water
flowing through the taps again. Nine days was
long enough to be without running water. We are delighted by
how easy life has become. The whole morning has been taken up
reorganizing all the buckets and big containers. I am refilling a lot
of them as we hear threats that the weather will return to the deep
cold in ten days. We might as well be ready. Meanwhile both the
kitchen and the bathroom feel so much bigger without all the lined-
up water containers.

1 January 2011—Two women in the shop were discussing which
newspapers are the best kind for getting the fire started. One of
them confessed that she had taken to using firelighters in recent
years but, what with money being tight, she was back to starting
the fire with paper and sticks. They both agreed that the colour
supplements were useless and that any kind of shiny pages were
not very good either. One of them swore by the *Irish Independent*
while the other preferred *The Nationalist*. *The Irish Times* and *The
Times* from England were about the same in terms of flammability,
but neither of the women bought these papers often. *South Tipp
Today* was a dependable favourite, and especially good because it
is free.

16 January—The days are getting longer. Every day is longer than
the day before. We all remark that there is A Bit of A Stretch In It.
The light seems to be changing faster and faster. The shortest day of
the year is the 21st of December, but locally the visible lengthening
of days is measured from the 6th of January. They call this The
Cock's Step. Every little amount of extra daylight is determined by

the length of his step. I am told that there is one minute and a half of extra light every day. I do not know exactly how this is translates into the distance of The Cock's Step, but I assume he is rushing and therefore his steps would naturally be elongated.

19 January—A group of very small children was being lined up on the footpath. Two women from the day care centre had the children pressed up against my car. They were all stroking the glass and making cooing noises through the window. Em had climbed from the back of the car up and into the passenger seat. The children were talking to her and patting the window as if she might feel their pats. Because I had parked close to the curb, they had a little height from the elevation of the footpath and they could look her in the face. She kept her head very close to the window and watched them quietly as they played at stroking her. When I saw what was happening, I offered to let Em out of the car so that the children could pet her. One of the woman said "No, don't even think of it! They would be terrified. This is much better. It is like she is on the television."

26 January—The lean-to has collapsed with the weather. This is not the big lean-to but the extra lean-to that was built onto the side of the big lean-to last year. At that time we needed more storage space for the firewood. Now the extra lean-to has been emptied of firewood. In the order of firewood rotation, it was time to use that supply. Perhaps the wood was holding the little lean-to in position. Now it has collapsed and I do not see any reason to rebuild it. No longer a useful structure, it is just pieces of wood and an old window.

29 January—We are all worried about Teresa Murphy. I stop by many mornings as Em and I walk past. I speak to whomever is in the kitchen. Sometimes it is one of her two sisters and sometimes it is Seamus. Sometimes it is Teresa herself. The early prognosis of the cancer was that it was discovered too late and that Teresa would not live until Christmas. Her two sisters came over from England and one of their husbands came too. The sisters are there to try to make daily life easier and to try to make life fun. Teresa's son and daughter-in-law from Fermoy drive up often. On Christmas Eve they

arrived with their three children and everyone slept in sleeping bags all over the house. They lit Chinese lanterns in the backyard and sent them up into the darkness of the night with wishes tied to them. On New Year's Eve, the family returned with their sleeping bags and everyone danced a Conga line through the house.

In early January, Teresa got a new wig. She looks very youthful and lovely with it. Some days she looks so good, we all forget that she is ill. On other days she cannot get out of bed.

3 February—A man came by to cut down Teresa's apple tree. She said she just could not bear the mess of the apples all over the ground and she had to have the problem eliminated and she had to have it done now. It was a mission about cleaning house and she would not be deterred. I reminded her of how beautiful it is when the huge old tree is covered with blossoms every spring. One of the sisters said, "Yes, but it does not last long, does it? Any old wind comes along and it is all over."

The man was revving up his chain-saw as I left. As I write this, I know that the tree is now cut up into pieces to be dried for firewood. The pieces are already piled up in the shed. There are no other trees in Teresa's yard. There are bushes and shrubs, and there are mature trees around the edges of her land. There are no trees to compare to that old apple tree. I shall miss it.

5 February—Wind. Wind. Wind. It feels like these loud winds have been here forever. I think it is actually only three days. The sound is constantly in our heads. We can hardly sleep for it. Now we have heavy rain along with the winds. I am back into my supply of rubber shoes. Actually I am never far from my supply of rubber shoes. Some people have lots of designer shoes and boots. They have party shoes and city shoes and country shoes. I have lots of rubber footwear. I have very rough rubber boots to wear in the garden, and I have tall rubber boots to wear when walking through fields. I have rubber clogs in three or four different styles. Some of these rubber shoes I wear if I am going to the shop but some others I don't wear anywhere but here. There is one pair of rubber clogs that I wear only back and forth to the sauna once a week. It would be great if I loved rubber, but I do not. I appreciate rubber for its usefulness. It would be awful if I had only canvas or leather shoes. There would be long stretches of the year when my shoes would never be dry. The trouble with rubber shoes is how very hot my feet get while wearing them.

I wore my wellington boots to yoga class one wild and wet night. The women at class were aghast that I would appear in town wearing muddy rubber boots. I think everyone in modern Ireland now lives in houses surrounded by tarmac and gravel. The aspiration is to never have mud on one's shoes. I do not know if this is just a practical consideration or if it is about not living like one's grandparents.

7 February—The general election is in full swing. Posters and signs are everywhere. Our local TD has left his party and is running as an Independent. He is hoping to distance himself from the destruction his party wreaked upon the country while in office. His vans are everywhere. They are all covered with pictures of his head as well as his name and his slogan. Because the vehicles are visible wherever we go, there is the impression that Mattie himself is racing around the countryside. We know that he has a large family and an enormous extended family. These vans are being driven by many different people. and are being parked here and there, always in highly visible spots. They function as mobile signage. Mattie himself is not everywhere, but his name and his face are.

One bit of campaign advice that all parties are agreed upon is that you cannot win an election in this country without going to funerals.

12 February—There is a new drive-in movie theatre in Cork. When it opened a few months ago, it was heralded as the biggest drive-in movie theatre in Europe. I am not sure, but it might also be the only drive-in movie theatre in Ireland. One of its offerings is an awning device which covers each motor car. Once the vehicle is under the awning, it does not matter if it starts to rain because the awning will keep the rain off the car. The awning means that the driver never has to turn on the windscreen wipers. Windscreen wipers would be a serious detraction from film viewing. The outdoor screen is huge. These days many people have large flat screen television sets in their homes. People can sit on their sofas and watch film action which is as large or larger than real life. If four or more people go to the new drive-in theatre they will be squished into a motor car together. The people in the back seat will be straining to look around the heads of the people in the front seat. And everyone will be looking through a windscreen at a great big screen down the hill. I think that looking through the windscreen will reduce everything back to the size of a smaller television than

most of these people have at home. I have not heard much more about the new drive-in since the excitement of its opening. I wonder if it is getting much business. I wonder if it is getting any business.

10 March—The starlings are back. They are beginning to build their nests in the barn. It seems very early for this activity but I think that I think this every year.

12 March—The daffodils are fully up and there are buds ready but most of them are not in flower yet. Every year I intend to plant some early flowering bulbs but then every year I forget, and my blooms are all a bit later coming up than everyone else's. This means that my daffodils are still flowering long after most of them have long gone. I get to enjoy them all. Ideally, some early ones and some later ones would provide a long and beautiful growing season. Perhaps this year I will remember but the chances are that when the autumn and bulb planting time arrives, I will again be thinking of something else that needs to be done. At least my daffodils are in big amorphous swathes and not just in some straight lines along the edge of a fence or a bed. People seem frightened to have their blossoms in clouds and clumps throughout grassy areas. Everything is controlled about the growing of local daffodils which I guess allows everyone to mow their lawns like mad well before the daffodils have died back. Or maybe there is not such a love of the word swathe. I love the word swathe. Regimentation takes a lot of the pleasure away from the yearly arrival of daffodils. I like being surprised by them every year. I especially like how the patches of blossoms make me walk from barn to barn in different routes. Getting across to the sauna is especially circuitous.

15 March—The bottle banks down in the village are in the car park next to the church. It is often tricky to arrive with a load of bottles and jars for throwing into the recycling containers and to find the car park unexpectedly full of cars. If a funeral or some sort of church service is going on, it feels rude to start smashing the bottles. It is not a job

which can be done quietly. I really hate returning home with all my rattling glass.

Em loves going along for the Glass Crash. She likes the car park when it is empty. She follows smells all around the edges of the paved area. Then she goes up onto the grassy place by the stream where there are a few picnic tables. There is a lot of smelling to do since this is where many local dogs come to walk. In good weather there is also the possibility of dropped food. If I stop with just a small number of things to smash, I am finished too quickly and she has not had time for her full exploration. On these occasions it is difficult to get her back into the car. This is my excuse for leaving the bottles and jars to really add up and then when I take a huge load down, Em has plenty of time for her investigation of village smells.

17 March—I saw a few of the parades around the country on the six o'clock news. My favourite marchers this year were a swim team in Waterford's parade. The team was a group of little boys, aged about ten or eleven. They flapped down the street wearing flippers and with their arms swimming along through the air in what looked like a crawl stroke. The boys worked quite hard to roll their heads and practice rhythmic breathing as they flapped along.

21 March—After all these weeks, the smell of something dead and rotting still lingers in my studio. It might be a new dead thing or it might be the same old dead thing. It is not too bad as long as I can leave the door open but the weather remains normal for March. Normal means a sunny and bright afternoon accompanied by a sharp and bitter wind. The cold wind forces me to close the door and then I am trapped inside with the smell. I have a little device which uses a candle to heat some lavender oil diluted with water. The lavender scent does not remove the smell of decay; it only covers it up. Today the afternoon sun was bright and it was not too cold. I had the door open and everything was pleasant. I heard Joe going back and forth on his tractor in the fields. After a while the stench of fresh slurry

filled the air outdoors. He was spreading slurry and the slurry was spreading its smell. I could not keep the door open any longer. The smell inside and the smell outside were all horrible.

26 March—Em had a small bone at lunchtime today. As always, she takes it outside. She went to the same place on the grass where she always goes to eat a bone or any special treat which demands some time and concentration. With a bone, she drops it onto the grass and then rotates her head very slowly in each direction. She looks around for several minutes just to be sure that no one is going to steal her bone. Maybe I am wrong about this. Maybe it is not about being robbed. Maybe she would like someone to see that she has this treasure. Maybe she would like to sense their envy and to feel that she has to protect her bone. Maybe she is longing for an audience.

Once she settles into the eating, she does not look around again. Sometimes I tease her by taking the bone from her. She does not snarl or lunge for it. She is both gentle and trusting. She watches the bone and looks at me with a terrible sadness and confusion, which, of course, makes me give it back immediately.

27 March—Last night we moved the clocks forward an hour. Between 8.30 and 9.30 on Saturday evening was proclaimed Earth Hour. Everyone was asked to turn off their lights for that hour. We planned to eat dinner during that time. We got the food ready by candlelight and lit the dining table with candles. It was very pleasant to sit quietly. It felt darker and quieter than usual. We often eat by candlelight, but there was not even a light coming in from the kitchen. This darkness felt darker and softer.

When Em could wait no longer, she started to nudge me and when I could stand her nudging no longer, I took her down for the meadow walk. I decided to go without even a torch to guide me and I thought for sure that all the lights on houses off across the valley would be turned off. I went out expecting distant darkness. I assumed that everyone would be participating in the one hour with no electric light. Some houses were dark and I like to think they were participating, but maybe they were just not at home. Several houses in the far distance were lit up with their outside lights as usual and they were probably not home either.

28 March—I spoke to an elderly man down in the village. He tried to tell me a long and complicated story but he kept forgetting big

portions of the plot. Getting confused made him angry and that got him more flustered. When he could not remember the name of the woman who was essential to the narrative, he attempted to describe her. He hoped that his description would help me to arrive at her name. He finally said, "You know her—of course you do. She is a small woman. She is like you yourself. She is low to the ground."

30 March—We save all our paper off-cuts. I always believe they will be useful for something. I have had to concede that there are just too many long narrow pieces of paper. Nobody needs this many bookmarks. There were so many of these off-cuts collected on one shelf that I decided the shelf would be better used for something else. Each tidy pile of hundreds of strips of paper was held together with two or three elastic bands. I gathered together all the piles and tried to think what I should do with them. Of course, I could take them to be recycled. Then I thought to offer them first to the day care centre in the village.

I stopped there this afternoon. I showed them to Marie with an apology because I realized that most of the paper was white although there were some shades of brown. There were not many bright primary colours to excite little children. She gasped and said, "Oh my god, no, they are perfect. We are making birds' nests. These are perfect. Perfect."

18 April—I had not seen the postman since I returned from America. When I went out to collect the post this morning, he welcomed me home and asked me about my father. I was touched that he remembered the reason for my trip. When I said that Dad was not doing very well, I got choked up. I said that my father was actually terrible and that there was no chance for him to ever get better. He squeezed my arm. He spoke of losing his own mother and he said to me, "You will never get over this."

19 April—The census woman came down to collect the census form today. According to the instructions, all the forms were supposed to be filled in on the evening of Sunday 10 April. She said that many people have still not filled in theirs yet. The census woman was convinced that there was no worry in it and that they would surely have them done by the end of the month. I asked if that did not defeat the idea of everyone doing it on the same day. She said there was no harm in it and she felt that the same month was nearly as good as the same day.

I did not tell her what one man said to me about the census. He said, "They only want to know Yes or No, so whatever the question, it is best to say No."

21 April—I've learned two different springtime pishogues in the last few days. First though, I had to be told that a pishogue is the Irish word for a spell or a superstition.

One of these is that if you bury a hard-boiled egg in the soil of your neighbour's potato patch before Easter, your neighbour (the victim) will have a wretched potato crop. The crop of yourself (the perpetrator) will be blight-free and plentiful. I do not know if the hard-boiled egg is supposed to be still in the shell or if it should be peeled before it is buried.

The second pishogue is that it is bad luck to pick primroses and bring them into the house before Easter. This one was explained to me as I was marvelling at the hundreds of them growing down the boreen this year. With so many growing wild, it has never been a flower I thought to pick and bring into the house anyway.

23 April—A pitcher full of wild garlic sits on the table. The flowers are bright and white and they look like exploded stars against the soft green leaves. I can never decide which smells stronger, the leaves or the flowers. I like seeing them and smelling them here inside the house but mostly I love walking through them outside. Then their tasty smell is on the walk with me.

26 April—Today we were offered a dead hare by some friends. They had been given the hare by someone else, but they don't want to eat it. They had offered it to various other people but not one person wanted to eat it. We asked why no one wanted it.

There is a superstition that the hare is an animal with magical powers. I could not be sure if the superstition included the fact that, because of its magical powers, it should not be eaten, or if the idea of magical powers just put people off. We described various rich and delicious hare dishes from different cultures. We suggested that perhaps the magic of the hare would be passed on when it is eaten. None of our enthusiasm had an effect. The real power of the hare was such that our friends were not going to eat it. We said we would be delighted to take the hare off their hands. We shall have to be careful who we invite to eat it with us.

27 April—I was driving up the narrow road. Far up ahead I could see a cow weaving from side to side. Then I noticed a farmer walking along in his high Wellington boots beside the car. I rolled to a stop and wound down the window. He ignored the window and hopped into the car beside me. I said, "She's a frisky one." He said, "Yes." Very slowly, I drove up towards the cow. She started to rush away but then suddenly veered left and into the space of a gate. I pulled the car up just a little beyond her and in at an angle to cut off

 further escape in the wrong direction. The farmer said "Thank you," got out of the car and went after the cow. I continued up the road. I could see them both in my rear view mirror. The cow was running far ahead of the farmer again, but now she was running downhill and in the right direction.

2 May—Maurice the Gloomy Donkey is gone. He has not been in his meadow for a week or so. The gate is open. Maybe he has been taken back to join the other donkeys. Perhaps he has been sold or traded or given away. Maybe he is being used for the function of reproduction. He has been so unpleasant, I shall not miss him. Em no longer even turned her head towards him as we passed.

6 May—This morning is beautiful with a kind of watery sunlight spread over everything. The sky looks too white to be sunny. The white looks a lot like the white of skimmed milk, or of milk diluted by water. But there are patches of dark green on the fields where trees are throwing out shadows on the bright grass. After two solid days of lashing rain, this tentative sunlight is very welcome. All the greens are greener than they were and the ground is squishy underfoot. After so many, many weeks of dry, hot weather, the soil was hard. The growth of everything had slowed down. Now things are growing even as I watch. Spring has arrived for the second time. The birds are noisy and busy. I am glad to hear the sound of the Telephone Birds. As with all my bird identification, I do not have the proper name to give these birds. I am not even sure what the bird

who makes this noise looks like. I call it the Telephone Bird, but in these days of so many different kinds of rings on so many different kinds of telephones, this one sound might not be so distinctly a telephone sound to anyone else but me.

10 May—My father is dying. He is dying as I sit here. He is dying all day. The phone calls go back and forth over the ocean. I am so far away. There is nothing I can do. The rain has been on and off all day. It rains hard and then it stops. The sun comes out, then it clouds over and it rains again. I am here and he is there. Joe arrived on his tractor to gather up the cows. From this far field to the milking shed is almost a kilometre. I guess that is about two thirds of a mile. Cows walk slowly. They walk steadily but they walk slowly. It takes them a good while to walk that distance. The cows walked all the way down there and they were lined up and milked in turn. Now they have made the long slow journey back to this same field. The cows have returned and my father is still dying. All his medication has been stopped. There is morphine to make him comfortable. The rain starts again and then it stops again. When the sun comes out there is a rainbow. I know the rain will start again soon. There is nothing I can do. There is nothing anyone can do. It is all happening so fast. It is the slowest thing I have ever waited to have happen.

18 June—Today I was stopped by a neighbour's child. She wanted to show me the shiny cross hanging on a silver chain around her neck. She told me that she had received it as a gift for her First Holy Communion. She then stood up tall and, with the help of her fingers, she listed off her other gifts. She told me she got six Fifties, nine Twenties, seven Tens and a Fiver. It took me a few minutes to recognize that these were amounts of money. The word Fiver is what gave it away. I was a bit stunned. I did not know what to say. I thought the ritual was supposed to be about religion, but she never mentioned religion. Her interest was only concerned with acquisition. I guess that is probably a normal kind of kid thing. I told her she was A Very Lucky Girl. She said, "I know."

25 June—Em is walking a lot slower. As always, she is busy with many smells and examinations but her walking is not as fast as it used to be. Maybe her explorations of things along the way is just more thorough. It is hard for me because I like to walk at a good pace. In the boreen I have to walk more carefully and slowly, but

out on the tarmacadam road I walk really fast. When I turn and look back, Em is far behind me. I hate to just stop and wait for her, so I sometimes walk back towards her. This is confusing. She thinks this means we are turning around, so she stops and turns herself and then she is walking farther away from me, with me in the rear. My newest solution is to walk towards her but in a curve. I walk the curve of the road's width and then I make my curve into a large circle. If she is very far behind, I might get in five or even six circles or ellipses before she catches up with me. When I do too many of these loops, I get a bit dizzy but at least I do not have to stop walking. The more I elongate the circle, the less dizzy I get.

She now recognizes that this is just something I do along the way and it does not stop her forward movement. When she is slow, I call her a Slow Poke. Simon calls her a Slow Coach. It does not matter what we call her. She continues at her own speed.

27 June—We still have our Parish Pack. I cannot decide what to do with it. I was told of its arrival before it actually came. It is the brainchild of the new parish priest, Father Bobby Power. His area covers Ballybacon, Ardfinnan and Grange. I said that since we are not Catholics, it was perhaps not relevant to us. The woman telling me about it assured me that it was non-denominational. She said that it was just the new priest's way of introducing himself to everyone in the parish.

The fat envelope arrived, containing two colour images in ovals. One is of Jesus with a heart in his hand and 'Sacred Heart' printed below. The other is Mary, again with a heart in hand, and the words 'Immaculate Heart' printed below. We also received a set of rosary beads, and a folded and laminated card with all sorts of instructions about how to use the beads and do litanies and other things. Far from being non-denominational, this is a Propaganda Package. I am both fascinated and repulsed by its assumption that it is welcome here. Also included is a Parish Directory which mostly lists various religious events throughout the year and a bit of history about the diocese. There is a green census form which asks various questions about people in the house and about everyone's participation in various local activities, mostly religious ones. We have an opportunity to return the form in an envelope marked 'Confidential' to the Parish Office in Ardfinnan or to wait and perhaps someone will come to collect it.

Everything now is back in the envelope. There is not one single thing inside that I want. I have no interest in filling out this green form. I debate daily whether I should return the entire thing to Ardfinnan, or whether I should just throw it all away. Eventually, I shall become tired of seeing it on the table and the decision will be made.

28 June—I stood behind a woman while she was paying for her messages. This woman was complaining loudly about how useless her adult son has been to her since she was widowed. She said, "I would have been better off if it had been a lamb I'd given birth to all those years ago. At least then I could fatten it up and eat it."

2 July—We walked up the road to Teresa's house. It was a beautiful evening and we were pleased to be out in it. People were gathered in the house and in the backyard. Someone led us into the living room where Teresa was lying in her coffin. A young woman left as we came in. She said she was just in there because she did not want Teresa to be alone. There was not much pressure to stay in the room for long. I did not like seeing Teresa in her lavender outfit and heavy make-up. I did not like seeing her dead. We went back outside. Eventually the priest arrived and a great many people squeezed into the room and the hallway while various prayers were said and repeated. We were outside the front door, just far away enough to not hear too much of it. We stood in a loose group of people who all looked down at the ground or up and across to the Knockmealdown mountains. The early evening sun was glorious.

After that part was over, people ate and drank and talked. Many of the men were wearing short-sleeved shirts. It was a rare and perfect summer's evening. There were three little open-sided tents with chairs and tables and then a larger white tent with long tables full of sandwiches, cakes and more chairs. Down below the potato patch was another large tent which Teresa's son had put up. He and his wife and their three children had been sleeping there ever since Teresa died a few days ago. I think there are a great many people staying in the house.

At ten o'clock, we walked home without speaking. The sky was still bright. Everything was quiet.

3 July—Teresa's funeral was today. I was driving to the church in Grange but, as I neared the house, I saw a group of people waiting

 in the road and on the lawn of her house. I pulled over, got out and waited quietly in the sunshine with everyone else.

The six men carrying the coffin from the house could not fit through the gate while they were on each side of it. Another man stood in front and helped to lift the coffin higher and over the opening while the men squeezed through and got back into their positions and then they carried the coffin to the waiting hearse. Everyone followed in a long slow line of cars to the church.

The church in Grange is much nicer than many of the churches around here. It is not as bleak as most of them. I had not been there for a long time. The sunlight was pouring in. The church was full. It was a lovely turn-out for Teresa. There was a woman singing up in the balcony at the rear of the church which was unusual and pleasant. It was not quite the same as having hymns where everyone joins in but it was beautiful nonetheless. Everything proceeded as normal with a lot of standing, kneeling, sitting, more kneeling and repeating.

The singer was singing another song as two men came up the outside aisles carrying plastic colanders. These were brightly coloured colanders, as used for draining vegetables. They passed these down the rows of people and money was thrown in. I had no money with me. I only had my car keys. I have never seen a collection taking place at a funeral in any kind of church anywhere. A neighbour nudged me from behind and offered me her purse so that I could put something in the colander. I refused because I felt it was not right. I was even more convinced that it was not right when a bright orange colander was passed to Teresa's grieving family who were sitting in the front rows, sobbing and sad.

5 July—Anyone I meet while out walking or in the village, the first topic that comes up is the collection that took place at Teresa's funeral. I was correct to think that it is not a normal thing. Most people are outraged by it. They are upset too for the bereaved family. They are upset for those people who had no money and who might have felt embarrassed by it. Most people have a best suit but it is not the suit in which they keep any money in the pockets. Not one person has commented upon the plastic colanders. These must

be what is normally used for collections at a regular mass, so they do not even notice them. For me, they were astonishing. They were the very first thing I mentioned when I got home.

7 July—The swallows have made a nest in the tool shed. Simon found them annoying. It was tiresome to have bird droppings on every single thing in the place. He boarded up the gap above the door where they were entering and exiting. I was worried because if the eggs or even the babies were already in the nest inside the shed, the mother would no longer be able to get to them. The mother might be trapped outside while the babies were trapped inside, waiting to be fed. Simon removed the board and now we are learning to live with the mess. The young ones should be off and away soon. We hope.

The biggest challenge is remembering to bend from the waist immediately upon opening the door. The mother dives directly at whomever opens the door. It is essential to duck. Then she swoops out and away. I do not think she wants to attack. She is protecting her young. She is just warning us.

13 July—A friend's elderly mother has been suffering with Alzheimer's for several years now. She gets worse and worse. She will never get better. It is difficult for the family to stand by and to feel so helpless. Last week the mother started weeping. She was desperate to see her own mother, who was long dead. She simply would not be consoled. The weeping went on and on. The only option was to try to distract her from this impossible idea. My friend took her mother to the car wash. The suds and the water and whirling brushes were all very exciting from inside the car. The car wash proved to be a perfect distraction.

23 July—Last week a chimney sweep came to see about cleaning our chimney. He looked at our woodstove and asked questions and then he said it would have to be done From the Top Down. Since it was raining, he said he would not even consider going up onto the roof. He told us a great many dire things about the kind of chimney arrangement we have, saying that we were foolish to have not had the chimney cleaned even once in sixteen years. He said he would phone us next Sunday and arrange to come by on Monday, if the weather was dry.

We heard nothing, so we eventually phoned him back. He said he could no longer do chimneys From the Top Down. He had had one fall a few years ago and he didn't want to climb any more. He gave us the name of another chimney sweep who was happy to work From the Top Down.

Today two men arrived. One was very young and one was older. The older man said he had broken his leg fourteen times by falling off roofs over the years. He himself no longer did From the Top Down. He said that is why he had the young lad with him. The young one was happy to do it. He was fearless about climbing. He went up his ladder and he shoved brushes down the chimney while the other man was inside the house. They shouted back and forth to each other. The man down below had an enormous vacuum cleaner. I thought that the room might get dirty with the soot being pushed down, but he mostly used a little opening at the bottom of the brickwork. He had a sealing device that kept the soot being sucked right into the machine and not into the room. The room was left clean but smelling like some horrible cleanser which he used on the floor as well as on the inside of the stove.

The whole time the vacuuming was being done, the young lad was walking back and forth on the ridge of the roof. He pulled weeds out of the other chimneys which we are not using. He shouted down advice to us about how the chimneys should be sealed up to keep out the damp. The lad was extremely tall and skinny, and he walked around as calmly as if he were on level ground. It was terrifying to watch him.

Before they left, the older man told us that back in the days when he still did From the Top Down, an elderly lady asked him to paint her chimney quickly since he was already up on the roof. She gave him a gallon of paint and he painted and painted and was shocked at how much paint the chimney seemed to be absorbing. The quick paint job was taking him a long time. She came out of the house and said she was worried. He thought she was worried that he was using all the paint. She said yes she was a little worried about the paint but she was more worried that if he fell he would break her slates and she would have a hard time getting similar ones to replace the breakage.

28 July—There is a sign at the recycling depot. It is a printed sign near to the bottle banks. It reads NO CERAMICS AND NO DELPH. Once this would have confused me. Now I know that china plates and cups and bowls are all called delph. This is an evolution of language from Delftware, which is the blue and white patterned china which was prevalent for many years. Delftware originally

came from the town of Delft in Holland. Now everyday china comes in many colours, patterns and combinations and from many places. But here, all china is called delph and after supper or after breakfast or after dinner it is always important to wash the delph, to dry the delph and to put it all away before the next meal.

7 August—The fourteen blackthorn sticks are back on the wall. They were away. Now they are back and they look exactly right where they are. They were Willie English's sticks and now they are here in what was once his home. They look as if this is exactly where they belong, although I do not know what Willie himself would think of his out of doors sticks being presented like this inside the house.

8 August—Every year in August, there are two weeks that are traditionally the holidays for tradesmen. All the bricklayers, blocklayers, plasterers, carpenters, roofers, decorators, plumbers, joiners, electricians, and so on have the same two weeks off. The timber yards are closed. Many hardware and plumbing supply places are closed. I think the idea was that if everyone had the same time off, then no one would miss the work or hold up anyone else's work. I think this is that two weeks right now. This year it is particularly difficult to know because all the building work has already stopped all over the country. Since so very many people have no work, there is not going to be the same sense of a holiday. The quiet has been here for a while.

10 August—Last week in the paper there was a front-page story about a local man who had been arrested for sexual assaults on young children over some thirty-five years. The area of the article was underprinted with a soft gray to make it stand out from other pieces. The article was diplomatic. It did not mention the name of the village where the man lived, nor did it mention the name of the man. This was all to protect the victims. The article did cite the man's age and it described him as a pensioner who cannot afford to pay his bail, so he is being kept inside in the jail. When he was picked up by the gardaí, he was dressed in an open-necked shirt and a dishevelled pinstriped suit. It is a pretty specific portrait and locally we all know exactly who is

being described. Everyone is being very discreet and everyone is not discussing any of this. No one knows who the victims, both male and female, are and no one wants to make it worse for them. It is the biggest story not being discussed.

11 August—Em and I are varying our walks. One day we do the short Perimeter Walk and one day we do our usual Around Walk. This variety seems to agree with her and we are making better speed on the longer walk. Today I was caught short and I was desperate for a pee. I tried to walk faster but I soon realized that I was not going to make it home. There was too far to go and I just couldn't wait. I hopped over a gate and squatted down out of sight behind the ditch. Em wiggled under the gate and came and squatted exactly beside me. We peed together. It was a very companionable moment. It is not the first time I have been caught short and it is not the first time that she has sat down beside me. It is not the first time I have marveled that she knows exactly what I am doing and that she chooses to join me.

17 August—I am now an Irish citizen. I do not feel any different. I did not really expect to feel any different, but I remind myself that now I am Irish, and European.

The ceremony took place at the Garda training college in Templemore. It was a larger event than I'd anticipated. There were 300 people there from 53 different countries. I sat between one young man from Eritrea and another from Brazil. A family from the Sudan were in the next seats. Those seeking asylum paid no money for their citizenship. The rest of us did. There were many tears. For so many of these people, it is the first time in a long time, or maybe ever, that they have rights. The possibility of a passport gives them the freedom to travel in safety. I did not expect to be so moved by the whole thing.

We were separated from our one guest each. We sat on blue chairs up front and our guests sat farther back in the gymnasium on black chairs. We had red ribbons around our necks. The guests had black ones. We had to wait quite a long time for the ceremony to begin, so the Garda brass band played various tunes, mostly a medley of Beatles songs. The assembled people kept jumping up and taking photographs of each other with their new

Certificate of Citizenship held up in front of them, and even of all of us in the crowd. Our certificates were given to us in a clear plastic envelope and every single person held their envelope up in front of them for the photos. I did not see one person taking the certificate out of the envelope to be photographed more clearly. After a little while, and because the wait was so long, everyone started rushing up and having their photos taken on the stage. We were all wearing little enamel pins of the Irish flag. The woman who presented them to each of us told us that the Minister for Justice and Equality wanted us to wear them during the ceremony. She made each request sound very personal: "The Minister would like You to wear this pin". As a group, we had to swear fidelity to the Irish state, and we had to listen to a little speech. As part of the swearing of fidelity, all 300 of us read out our own name and our own address from our own piece of paper at the exact same time. It was a moment of complete cacophony.

After the ceremony, we all filed out and went into the huge cafeteria used by the Garda trainees. There was a table set up with tea, scones and some cakes. The serving of the tea and cakes was chaotic. They ran out of things to eat before everyone had had any. They ran out of things before much of anyone had had any. We have all lived long enough in Ireland to know that many organized things are bit of a mess. There were several ladies marching off to a kitchen somewhere far in the back and returning with a pot of tea which served only about seven people. Then they had to make the long trip again.

No amount of tealessness stopped the cheerful atmosphere, the endless posing with certificates or the phone calls to family and friends who had not been allowed to attend. As we drove away, everyone in the other cars or walking or waiting for the bus waved like mad to each other. We were all the best of friends for the day.

21 August—After she has had her walk down the meadow and has eaten her little night snack, Em has taken to going outside again. She likes to lie by the back door with her head moving slowly from side to side. She looks out into the darkness and gives the impression of being ready for immediate action. I call this doing Night Dog. It is ironic because Em often spends most of the day sleeping and not paying attention to anything or anyone. As Night Dog, she is alert and ready. When I go to the door to see if she is ready to come in, she turns to look at me, shows me the whites of her eyes and goes back to looking out at the night.

24 August—The car mechanic always reminds me that I am not from here. It has become a bit of a game with him. When I say two thirty, he says half two. Then I ask if that isn't what I just said, he says, "No, you said two thirty. Here it is half two."

10 September—The fig tree has really suffered with the cold over these last two winters. This spring I was sure we had lost it for good. I broke off a lot of dead branches. They were too dead for me to even need a saw. Some very pathetic but hopeful ones remained. It took a while for any leaves to form. A few hard little figs appeared over the summer but they never reached maturity. Today I snooped around under the big leaves and found one perfectly ripe fig. We cut it in half and shared it. It tasted of warm places. It was perfect and not at all woody. One Fabulous Fig.

13 September—The winds are less strong but it is still breezy. I thought it might be a perfect day for drying laundry but there is still a strong enough wind to flip the clothes around and around the line until they are no longer blowing in the wind. I have been out to untangle them a few times but now I'll just leave them and hope the sun dries them even in their wadded-up state.

Most of the older places around have a stone shed of some sort which gets used for many things. One of the uses is for drying laundry. The shed is usually open on one long side, so that the wind can come in and blow around but the roof keeps the rain off. This way people were able to get their clothes and sheets mostly dry even in the wettest of weather. No one builds sheds like this for any of the new houses. Some people have a garage which houses anything except a car. Some people have a small wooden shed for garden tools, and maybe their stuff for recycling. There is no need for the old drying line in an open shed anyway because I think most people have clothes driers.

14 September—One good thing about the onset of colder weather and chilly nights is the diminishing possibility of stepping on a slug when I get up in the night in bare feet.

21 September—There is still a lot of stuff to collect: blackberries, wild damsons, blotcheens, several kinds of rosehips, apples, elderberries, and field mushrooms. Everything is plentiful but there is just not enough time in a day to gather it. And the picking is only one thing. Once the picking is done, there is the need to do

something with it all. Freezing things or making jams and cordials is time-consuming. I waver between feeling that I should use every single thing and not waste the bounty, and wanting to get some other things done. I have taken to carrying a bag when I walk with Em. As she is often slow and lagging far behind, I can stop at any moment and gather blackberries. They are everywhere. I come back from each walk with a good supply.

22 September—Hector, the golden retriever, was in the middle of the track as I was driving out this morning. He looked at me and at the car but he did nothing to get out of the way. There was not really enough space for him to squeeze between the car sides and the bushes, but he did not even look as if he would try. I got out and went to talk to him. I saw that he had a chain attached to his collar. The chain was long and connected to a wooden post. The post was big and heavy and he was obviously tired from having pulled it along for as far as he did. He had escaped from being tied up by pulling the post out of the ground and away with him. I picked up the post and carried it in both arms. It was taller than me, very heavy and awkward to carry. The dog walked calmly along behind me still attached to his chain and therefore to the post. As we got closer to the farmyard, Hector got excited and started to run home. Our positions were reversed. I had to run in a staggering kind of way, barely able to keep up with my heavy burden.

24 September—The village has been divided. The county council is doing some work on the little bridge which goes right through the middle of the single thoroughfare. They have closed the road to all but pedestrian traffic. People in cars are trapped on one side or the other. It's not possible to buy petrol or to get a tyre repaired if you come in from the wrong side. It is not possible to drive to the post office or the hardware shop if you come from the  other way. People who are on the opposite side from the side we enter from now have a long roundabout journey by car just to get to Clonmel. There are routes through Ardfinnan or up and around on the mountain roads just to get to places that are normally quite near. It is all confusing and since there was no warning, a lot of people are angry. There is a lot of walking up and down the road

which is good to see. People park on one side and walk along to get to the things on the other side. Everyone is talking a lot to everyone else, even if it is only to complain. We are told that the repairs will be finished in three weeks, but everyone is grumbling that that probably means it will not be done before Christmas.

27 September—I was walking up the boreen with Em. I looked down and saw what I assumed was a little dead mouse. I almost stepped on it. It was a small and very young creature. It was grey, like a mouse, but it had a long nose, like a little snout. I decided it must be a baby shrew. They always look prehistoric. Ten steps along there was another one and a few more steps along there was a third. If some other animal had raided their nest, I think it would have eaten these babies. I could not see any signs of blood or wounding. It was just three dead shrews all in a row on the way up the track. Maybe they were running away from something or maybe they were just running. Cause of death unknown.

17 October—There was a message on the answer phone asking us to be on the look-out for a Friesian heifer which had escaped from someone down the road. I was pleased that anyone thought we would recognize a Friesian heifer from any other kind of cow.

23 October—Desperate, torrential rain all day long. Even for here, it has been unbelievable. We drove up into the mountains to have lunch with a friend who lives in a large crumbling castle. It was

cosy and dry inside but the sound of the rain on the roof was incessant. As we drove home, the water was rushing off the mountains and down the roads. It felt as if we were in a too small boat on a deep and dangerous river. There were no puddles on the road. The road was just all water. It was hard to see where the road ended and if there was any land at all on either side.

My car window had been left open a tiny bit while we were visiting. I found myself sitting in a huge puddle as I drove. My feet were splashing in water as I used the pedals. I was soaked from the waist down by the time we got home. The phone is dead. The winds and the rain continue.

24 October—Thursday is Polling Day. My voter registration card arrived this morning. We are choosing a new president and also deciding on two referendums. This is my first time voting in a national election. Up until now I could participate only on very local issues. Now, as a citizen, I have full privileges.

A few weeks ago Simon received a notice about his postal ballot. He went into the county council office and said that he did not need an absentee ballot because he is here, and will be here on the 27th to vote. Last February, when there was a general election, he needed an absentee ballot because he was going to be out of the country on polling day. He had a form which he had to take to the Garda Station to have his identity validated. Then a paper was sent to him here so that he could fill it in and return it. Now the council has told him that since he had an absentee ballot earlier in the year, he must have one again. No one is allowed to be absent for less than a year. He went again to the Garda Station and again had someone sign a paper saying that he is himself. Then the ballot papers came by post to the house and he voted and posted them back.

There may be some logic in all of this which we are missing. If you are absent for a year, why on earth would the ballot be sent to your own house? Surely you would not be there to receive it.

28 October—I went to collect Simon off the bus in Ardfinnan. I went a bit early to walk with Em along the river. There are always several flocks of ten or fifteen geese walking along in the field or swimming. Em is not interested in them, nor are they interested in her. They are lovely to see, but the area all along the river edge gets very slippery with the huge amount of goose droppings. At one point Em decided that she had to have a swim, so she hopped off the bank and into the river. She chose a steep drop-off point and when she turned to climb back up, she could not do it. The mud was slippery there. It was too steep and there were reeds tangling around her. She did not bark or whimper. She just kept trying and trying to scrabble up. The more she struggled, the less possible it looked. I squatted down and tried to pull her by her front legs. My squatting position gave me no leverage. I only just stopped myself from toppling into the water. My solution was to lie down flat on the ground and to pull her hard, using her front legs and her long hair to yank her up the banking. I got her up and out and she took off at speed to go back over the bridge. She stopped and waited for me at the far edge of the field. I was soaking wet and covered with goose shit, and I still had to wait for the bus to arrive.

1 November—Yesterday there was torrential rain and terrible wind all day long. I have seen a lot of rain since I have lived here but I do not think I have ever seen rain like that. Today it is raining still but not with quite the ferocity of yesterday.

Both today and yesterday we have been printing in the shed. Each time we moved from barn to shed or shed to house, we were rushing to get through the rain. It is difficult to walk slowly through this kind of downpour. Running seems essential. Wearing a hat or a coat does not help much since the wind whips everything around and the minute we go inside we are dripping onto something.

All morning we were getting phone calls from Seamus, the Eircom man, who was attempting to repair our telephone line. He was up the road, out in the rain, sawing at bushes and branches. He said the branches had rubbed the cables and torn a coating off them and that is why we had no service. He would telephone Simon on his mobile and then one of us would run into the house to try to phone him back on the land line but then it wouldn't work, so we would have to go back out and call him from the mobile. These calls went back and forth for several hours. Twice we thought the line was repaired but it wasn't. Finally it was fixed and Seamus was really wet. He left to go and see to some cables that had come down in the wind up near Ballinamult. He told us he would ring again tomorrow to check if it was still working. So far so good. After eleven days without, it is good to have the telephone working again.

20 November—There is always a bit of land between a fence, a wall or a ditch and the road. In some rural counties, these edges of the road are scruffy and bare, but in Tipperary the verges are lush and green with grass, weeds and growth. I assume that the land right up to the edge of the road belongs to the person who owns the adjoining fields. Maybe it is not really owned by anyone. Maybe it is an extension of the public road. This strip of land along the side of the road is called The Long Acre. The Long Acre is regularly used by the Traveling Community as a place to tether their horses for grazing. It is a delicate balance to give a horse on a rope enough length so that he will be able to reach plenty of the grass around him, but not enough to allow him out into the road where he might be hit by a passing car. The Long Acre offers free grazing with a modicum of danger.

28 November—If we are having tea with someone and the conversation is going along nicely, we might be offered A Hot Drop. A Hot Drop is that extra bit of hot tea added into a cup which is not yet empty. A Hot Drop extends the cup of tea and keeps the visit going a bit longer.

2 December—I drove Simon into Cahir this morning so that he could catch the train to Dublin. It was frosty and dark when we left the house. It was still dark when we got to Cahir. It felt like it was very late at night but it wasn't. It was early morning. One shop was open on the corner. I stopped so Simon could hop out and buy a newspaper. While I waited for him, I saw two men down the street. They were the only people in sight. As I watched, they came closer to where I was parked. I saw that they were window cleaners. They had finished one pair of shop windows and they moved along with their buckets and their extended poles to begin the windows of another shop. I watched them working quietly and carefully together. I watched them washing windows in the dark. I wondered how they could know if the windows were clean. There was no light outside and there was no light inside. If there were smears or smudges, there was no way they could be seen.

Em and I went up onto the station platform with Simon. I was expecting it to be empty, but there were about twenty people waiting for the train. Em went and smelled the legs of everyone. Each person said hello and scratched or petted her. Then she came and sat down on the edge of the platform. I held onto her when the train pulled in. It was a small train. There were only two little carriages. There are always only two carriages. Simon got in with the other people and the doors closed and the train went away. Em looked and looked at the place where Simon had been standing before he entered the train. She could not see him nor could she see the place he had gone into. She found both his disappearance and the disappearance of the train disconcerting. He went in and the place he went into pulled away. She did not want to leave the platform without him.

10 December—Last night we received news that Max had died. We were shocked. He was a big healthy happy dog. How could he

have a heart attack and be dead in a few seconds? This afternoon we walked up to the house. Max was laid out on his bed in the porch. There were scented candles burning. He looked as if he was sleeping. He had that straight legged lie-flat look that dogs often have when they sleep. I wept to see him like that. Em sniffed him bit and then she went off into the house.

We sat down in the kitchen and drank tea and talked about Max. Another neighbour arrived and we all told stories with Max in them. He had been a rescue dog, so no one knew his exact age. They thought he was about eight. He had a few bad memories from his previous life. As a result, he did not like men with cigarettes, nor could he bear to be tied up. He hated going into sheds or any enclosed small dark places. Max was lucky that in his life here he was able to roam free. He loved to come for walks with Em and me. Most days I would whistle as we got near to his house, but sometimes he was waiting for us at the end of the drive. Coco was his good friend and he came to visit Max every morning. There was never any animosity between them as male dogs. Dogs and people all loved Max because Max loved everyone.

The family are going to bury him on Sunday morning out on the banking near to a place which they all love for its morning sun. They will plant some bulbs to mark the spot in the spring. I cried again when we left. I stroked Max and said goodbye but I could not see for my tears. I am crying again as I write this.

21 December—The path down into the meadow has become really slippery. It is the bit where the corner is sharp and the hill is steep. The mud can be deadly. It is the exact point where Em often catches up with me and races past at top speed barking into the night. If I am going to slip and fall anywhere, this is where it happens. Tonight I knew it was very wet and muddy so I decided to go around the opposite way. I walked down into the meadow on

what is usually our path for the upward and return journey. I did not worry about Em as she often takes off into the far field before running down to join me. When I was all the way at the bottom and she had not yet arrived, I whistled for her. I whistled and then I shouted and then I whistled again. I made so much noise that

I disturbed the birds sleeping up in the fir trees. They all came rushing out, flying around and making lots of noise. I whistled and shouted some more and then I walked back up to the yard. Em was sitting beside the vegetable bed moving her head from side to side and looking dejected. I called again but she did not respond. We have been wondering about her hearing of late. Now there is no doubt. She is deaf. It is sad.

24 December—I spoke to an older lady who wanted to know if I had heard some man singing on the radio. She could not remember his name but she felt that I should surely know him anyway. She said that he was a truly great singer. She said he was like a mix between James Brown and Pavarotti.

25 December—I feel sad every time Em and I walk past the house and Max does not come out to join us. Today Coco came down the drive. He is still stopping there each morning to visit Max. I wonder how long he will continue this ritual. He and Em sniffed each other and both turned as though to give Max another chance to appear. If I am in the mood to feel sad, I can acknowledge an absence at almost every house I pass. There are not very many houses, but it feels like a lot of people and a lot of dogs are missing along the way. Max and Maisie, and Mary, and Kelly, and Snoopy, and Teresa and Seamus, and Sam, Topsy, Partner and Syd. The years go by and each one who is gone gets replaced or at least remembered less often.

31 December—We were walking along our usual morning route when Greg came along in the van and said hello. He asked where Em was. She was, at that moment, standing down in the stream waiting for me to throw her a stick. He said he was off to take Molly for a walk in the mountains and asked if we wanted to go too. I was not sure Em could do a big mountain walk but he said it was a gentle one-hour circuit and because we would park and begin at a high place there wouldn't be too much climbing. It was a mild morning, so I was not really dressed for the mountain. I did not even have a hat. He said he had extra gear, so Em and I hopped into the van and he drove up the New Line toward Cappoquin. He loaned me some gaiters, a hat and a waterproof coat. Everything was too big except the hat, but none of that mattered. It was lovely to be up there. The ground was soggy and we walked through a stream and meandered through the wet moorland. Molly raced around like a mad thing but Em was staid and steady. I was proud of her.

Every time we think she is an old dog, she surprises us again. There were lots of sheep scattered about the hillside, all with red paint markings on their backs, but both dogs politely ignored them. Just as we got back to the van, a steady drizzle set in. It was a wonderful walk to end the year. Em has been sleeping heavily and snoring loudly ever since we got home.

7 January 2012—The Farmers' Market will reopen on the 14th of January. We were in Cahir early today and we drove into the castle car park as usual. Looking down the way, we saw one small table with a dark red umbrella beside a parked vehicle. It was the Egg Man. I went over to ask him why he was there since there was no market today. He got out of the vehicle where he was sitting to be out of the cold wind. As always on a market day, he was wearing his sturdy well polished leather shoes. A few months ago I would have called them brogues but now I have learned that brogues have patterns of small holes punched into the leather. Not all leather lace up shoes are brogues.

The Egg Man said that he might as well be there because his chickens keep laying. He said his chickens do not know that there is a holiday. They do not know what day it is ever. They lay eggs, so he has eggs, so he has to sell eggs. One man had been by first thing and he had bought one and a half dozen. A woman had bought two dozen. He said he would not have any trouble selling the rest. I bought six eggs and wished him a Happy New Year.

10 January—The consolidation of several shops into one premises is another aspect of the current climate of austerity. The health food shop now has a wine shop in its back room. The wine shop used to be up around the corner. And the next door shop has been broken through and it is the now a version of the home furnishings shop which used to be called *Home Thoughts From Abroad*. I always found this a strange name for a shop selling organic paints and lovely cotton fabrics and things for the house. I do not know if they have the same name now, but they sell many of the same things. Now these three shops can trade in one place and everyone's rent is lower and they can even share staff. I understand that the wine man is only in there two days a week. The rest of the time, the health food shop handles any wine transactions.

12 January—I have a new address book and I have been very slow to start using it. I have been so slow that I cannot even call the new

book new any more. I need to sit down and copy the details of individuals from the old book into the new one. I should just do it one letter at a time so that it is not a big chore. Each time I begin, I find myself confronted with the name of someone who has died. As long as they are there in my book, I am reminded of them on a regular basis. It is a pleasant thing to be reminded of a friend who is no longer alive. It is unnecessary to copy their details into my new book,  but if I do not copy the name and the details into my address book, then I no longer come across these absent friends by chance. It is this side-effect of negating people which keeps me from completing my task.

15 January—One cannot pay for a horse on a Sunday. I do not know if this is considered bad luck for the horse, or for the new owner, or maybe for the person selling the horse. It is just a fact.

18 January—He is Like the Head Cut Off His Father. This is what I was told today when I commented on a young baby boy. I said he looked a lot like his dad. This was a much stronger way of saying the same thing.

21 January—Yesterday I took a wheelbarrow down to the stream to collect all the rubbish that has appeared during the winter months. There were empty plastic drinks bottles and food packets probably left upstream by the wood cutters last year. It has taken this long for the current and the weather to bring everything down here. There were some big plastic bags left over from farming stuff and bits of old rubber hoses and tubing and many things I cannot name. There has been a lot of damage to the culverts which direct the water under the path. Big branches and trees have been carried downstream and the force of them hitting the banking has caused a lot of destruction. My picking up of the trash is not really making much of an improvement but at least I do not have to look at human detritus every day when I pass. It will just be nature's mess. I waded around happily in my Wellie boots. Em was delighted that we were walking about in the water together.

16 February—In recent years, the banks have closed branches all over the country. They have closed many banks in both towns and villages. In place of the banks, they have installed cash machines. An ATM machine is good for some things but it cannot provide all services. This has been difficult for people in rural places. Now the banks are removing the ATM machines too. In some places, especially in the west, a person might have to drive ten or fifteen miles to get to a machine to withdraw some cash. This is particularly difficult for people who have no car. The reason for the removal of the cash machines is that so many of them are getting stolen. Thieves come in the night with a JCB and they smash the wall and take away the whole machine. First they steal a car and then they steal a JCB and then they steal the ATM. It is a big operation and it demands a fair amount of research and planning. It must be worthwhile because it has been happening quite frequently in these difficult times. I have not heard of any of the cash machine thieves being caught yet.

18 February—I was down in the barn. Em was lying just outside the door. She likes to be there so she can keep an eye on me through the glass door and also keep an eye on the rest of her world at the same time. I heard a thud on the glass which meant that a bird had flown into it. This happens often. The birds dash around at speed and glass is a confusing material. I went to take a look. There was a blue tit on the ground right beside Em's head. I watched from inside the barn. The bird was alive and shaking. Em looked at the bird carefully. Then she stood up and sniffed at the bird. The bird could not move because it was either wounded or badly dazed. Em sniffed and walked around the bird and then she threw herself back down onto the ground a few feet away. I would like to think that she moved away from the bird out of respect and consideration for a creature in pain. Instead, I think she moved away because she was afraid of it. I went outside and put the bird into a sheltered spot near the flowering currant bush. When I came out later, Em was back in her usual place and the bird had flown away.

22 February—Em is in great shape. She is running and walking and being a happy, energetic dog. She does not look or act like a thirteen

year old. Besides our morning walk, and whatever the weather, we go out every afternoon for Games in the Field. We usually choose the frisbee. She takes four or five long runs down the field to fetch and then she calls it a day and takes the frisbee to her little house. This means she has had enough and the games are over. Not long ago, these games went on for hours. It is a relief to have her worn out so quickly. She seems to have come to terms with her deafness and, instead of slowing her down and making her old, it is now just one thing about her. To get into the house, Em has taken to hurling herself against the back door. She may be deaf, but she is strong. Being deaf means that she cannot hear herself scratching to be let in, so this is her solution to the problem. It is still too cold to come into the kitchen to find the door wide open after she has let herself in.

23 February—The High Stool is a seat at the bar. When someone is headed to the pub for a drink, he will say "I'm for the High Stool."

25 February—Kathleen is The Cheese Lady at the market. Today she had a bucket of green olives on her stand. She said she doesn't like olives and she does not know anything about them, so she feels she cannot recommend them. The cheese-maker who supplies her with cheese for the market has had some trouble getting paid by one of his customers in the North. Suddenly he is being paid in olives. He is not very happy about this. He is a maker of lovely goat and sheep cheeses and he proudly sells both his own and other people's cheeses at several markets. Olives are not what he wants to be selling. Now he has so many olives that he has to sell them to try to recoup his money. That means Kathleen has to try to sell them too. Her lack of enthusiasm is not very encouraging. I did not see anyone buying the olives this morning.

29 February—Every day there is more growth to notice. I am seeing wild garlic, primroses, daffodils, celandine, crocus, and even blossom on a few trees. There are lots of other things along the boreen. They are the things that I always mean to look up when I get home but then I never do. The herbs are coming up too. Chives and parsley and sorrel are all well advanced. Yesterday we made a fresh pesto with the new growth from the tarragon and some garlic and walnuts. The young tarragon tasted fantastic. Tulips are starting to show too. I think the first green of the leaves pushing out of the ground looks a lot like a part of a dinosaur. I think this every year. It is an ancient sort of shape.

On the way down the meadow, right before the steep slippery corner, there is a cluster of tulip leaves showing among the rough grass. I emptied some large plant pots there last autumn. I was trying to fill a hole which was a dangerous hole at that location beside the path and I knew I'd fall into it some night. The tulip bulbs must have been in one of the pots. I do not know what colour they will be but I am looking forward to their blooming.

5 March—I am the self-appointed caretaker of Johnnie Mackin's house. The house is empty and it is falling apart more and more every year. There is very little glass left in any of the windows. Some of the wooden window frames are completely gone. The front door is made of two doors of equal size which open inwards. I can tell when people have been in and wandering around the place because they always leave the door on the right side open. I walk past the house every day with Em. Whenever I see the door open, I push through the brambles and go to close it. She rarely joins me; she sits on the track and waits. I secure the two parts with an old piece of metal rod which has loops at either end. I hook the loop of one end through one handle. The other end of the metal stays in its position on the other door handle.

The windows in each of the doors are broken. There is a large hole in the bottom of the left-hand door. It might be that it was kicked in or maybe the wood of the door has just rotted. Animals, people and birds all have easy access to the interior of Johnnie's house. I do not know why it is so important to me that the front door be closed, but it feels respectful. I shall continue to close it for as long as the door itself remains intact.

6 March—Another very icy morning. As soon as the daylight comes, the grass is wet. I do not think we can call it dew when it has been so cold but it is not really melted ice either. I met PJ as I walked up the hill and we spoke of the cold and the wet. He said he had been Agitating over at Donal's early this morning. He was surprised by how wet he got just walking across the field. I was surprised by the word Agitating. I could not imagine what he was up to. I asked what he meant by Agitating. He said he had been stirring up slurry in the tank so that when they were ready to do the spreading later today, the slurry would have a good consistency. Getting it ready in advance is called Agitating.

27 March—I am not really fond of forsythia. I like it as a word but I am not so fond of it as a shrub or flower. It always makes its way into the house at this time of year simply because it is in bloom and it is bright. Today there are a few small sprigs of forsythia in a little jar on the table. The jar sits beside a wooden platter holding four yellow pears. The combination of these things could not look more beautiful.

31 March—I went down to the shop this morning and returned with three newspapers, some milk and a pair of crutches. I borrowed the crutches for Simon. He has been hobbling around with a stick for a few days. He has been unable to put his right foot down onto the ground. His hobbling has been a bit wild and unbalanced and, even though I have tried to move things out of his way, it is dangerous. It is great that we can get crutches at the shop. We always joke that we can get anything we need at McCarra's shop. It is that kind of shop. The crutches have taken this to a new level. I mentioned the crutch loan to someone later and I was told that hospitals here are allowed to use crutches only once for if they give them to a second patient, they might get sued for providing used and faulty goods. I am shocked by the wastefulness of this. No wonder the health authority is in financial trouble. I was told that the once-used crutches are collected by charities who send them off to Africa.

1 April—The tulips I bought at yesterday's market are a beautiful deep reddish purple. I was so pleased to see them and to bring them home that I did not notice their leaflessness. Someone had carefully cut every single leaf off each tulip. Where there should be several wide floppy leaves on a stem, there were only tiny green triangles. The flowers looked naked and foolish in the vase. I could not make them look right, even though their colour indoors was even more lovely than it had been out of doors. This morning I went outside and gathered some long leaves from the spent daffodils in the grass. I cut a few wide tall leaves from the wild irises down by the stream. The combination of these added to the blossoms does not look right but it distracts from the lack of real tulip leaves.

10 April—I took Em to the vet and now she has antibiotics and cream and a plastic collar around her neck to keep her from licking and scratching her tummy. The collar looks like an upside-down lampshade. She is annoyed and unhappy with this arrangement. I am to leave it on her for at least five days. She cannot lie down in her bed and she keeps bumping into door frames with the edges of her apparatus. We go back and forth between feeling sorry for her and trying not to laugh because she looks so foolish. It is bad enough that she is deaf but now the vet tells me that she is half-blind. Bumbling around with this collar is an indignity too far.

11 April—A woman stood on the pavement telling another woman that she knew what was going on. She kept saying more and more things to try to explain that she was not someone to be easily fooled. Her voice got louder and shriller. As I moved away, the last thing I heard her shout was: "I didn't come down in the last shower."

13 April—I took Em around on the usual boreen walk this morning. She was eager to go. Even though she bumped into a lot of stones and branches and things on the way up the path, she was pleased to just be going. She developed a very particular way of dragging the plastic collar along through the long grass in order to get a good lick of water. I did not let her down and into the stream for her swim, but she was not too bothered about that. Any walk at all was at least something more interesting than thinking about what she had around her neck.

16 April—Tommie was very sad when I saw him today. He had been caring for a friend's dog. The dog mourned while her owner was away for a fortnight. She waited all day every day at the end of the track for her owner. Each night, she had to be carried down to the house because she would not come when called. She wanted to stay and wait for the return of her man. The dog would not eat her supper or her breakfast. She never ate a thing for the whole fortnight. She drank some water but she refused all food. When the man returned at the end of his time away, the dog was overjoyed. That night, she ate her supper with enthusiasm. Her supper was the same sized supper she was always given but her stomach could not hold it after two weeks of eating nothing. She ate happily, but later that night she died.

17 April—Tuesday morning is when the Circuit Court sits in Clonmel. I never think about the court being in session unless I try to park in the area near the courthouse.

There is very little parking available when the court is sitting. Today I found a spot on the quay. I walked up the street and saw the gardaí unloading a prison van. The men being led out of the van were all young and skinny and they all looked like one another. There were lots of gardaí around. Some were attached to the prisoners with handcuffs and some were not attached but were keeping an eye on the prisoners. Others were keeping their eyes on the crowd. A group of people were gathered on some high steps across from the courthouse. The people shouted out to the prisoners and some of them shouted and jeered at the gardaí. The people on the steps were dressed the same way as the prisoners. The people on the steps looked just like the prisoners. Everyone was wearing baggy track suit bottoms and hooded sweat shirts. As the prisoners were led into the courthouse, the group on the steps ran down and rushed across the street in order to get seats inside. There was a lot of chaos and a lot of noise. I turned around and decided to walk along a different street.

22 April—When we pay for something in a shop, the total is often just rounded up. Actually it is rounded down to the nearest euro. I like this. It feels both generous and unfussy. If the person paying is short a few cent, the cashier just says "Oh, that's grand, so." and rounds it off. They might say "Well, what have you got there?" and they will look at our change and say "That is close enough, so." If the total comes to 16 euro 49 cent, we may end up paying 16.35. We may end up paying Only 16.00. They would even prefer to take less money than for someone to have to break a bill. This does not happen in the bigger stores and supermarkets, but it is normal in local shops.

Today we noticed that even the Tax Office participates in this relaxed manner with money. On their forms it says DO NOT ENTER CENT. If a tax bill comes to 2,378.57 euro, it must be rounded off to 2,378.00 euro or to 2,379.00 euro. They do not want to be bothered by the cent either.

27 April—The butcher in Ardfinnan has a refrigerated storage place across the street from his shop. On one side, there is a hairdresser's shop which is called Curl Up and Dye. On the other side is the green and the playing fields. The storage place is a small free-standing

building made of cement blocks. The door is open all day long. There are carcasses hanging inside which can be seen from the road. There might be a freezer compartment in there too. The flat roofed building is not large. It is just the size of a room. The two butchers are in and out and crossing the road all day long. Sometimes they have to wait for a car or the bus to pass while they stand with a side of beef or a lamb hanging over their shoulder.

28 April—I am not very good about offering tea. The ritual here dictates that you offer tea and the person being offered the tea says No. Then you wait a little longer and you offer again. Again, the person being offered the tea says No. The third time tea is offered, the person being offered the tea says Yes. This goes for anything being offered, not just tea. I get annoyed with having to play this game. I tend to believe people when they say No. Sometimes I just announce that I make the offer only once, so they should say Yes if they do indeed want it. If people know me, they understand that they can say Yes immediately. The people I do not know very well are the ones for whom I sometimes feel I should play the game. Even children are conditioned to participate in this ritual. It is a form of politeness. People can go away hurt or hungry if they are not given the correct number of times to say No before saying Yes.

29 April—I throw a stick down into the stream for Em every time we pass. I have thrown a huge number of sticks into this stream over the years. I have only one place where I can stand so that she can see me doing the throwing. With her deafness, she needs to see the throw to know that it is happening. I still shout "On your mark! Get set! Go!" each time, but that is for me, not really for her. It is getting difficult because there is a branch that blocks my throwing area. If I hit the branch, the stick might get lodged into the branch. Or the stick might bounce off the branch and drop straight down and land on top of Em. I need to get the throw right to pass over or under the branch and to land in the water. What I should do is to take a saw and cut this branch back. This is something I think of every day but I never take the saw or wear the Wellington boots which I would need to stand in the stream to do the cutting. A new development of the stick ritual is that when Em comes up the banking and flattens herself out to crawl under the fence, she sometimes gets her stick stuck. If she cannot get her stick through the opening with ease, she goes back down the

banking and drops the stick into the water. Then she pounces on the stick and carries it back up the banking and under the fence.

30 April—An older woman who looks youthful might be called a Fresh Woman. Being called a Fresh Woman is a compliment. It might also be said of a woman that She is Fresh Enough.

3 May—I have been loaned a book about the history of the creamery in Ireland. I am not particularly interested in this history, but since the person lending me the book was so enthusiastic, I felt I should read it. On page 24, there was a caption for a photograph of "Molly O'Brien of Ballyorgan, County Limerick hand-milking in the 1950s". In smaller letters underneath, it was written "This is not the Molly O'Brien mentioned in the text". I was intrigued by the double presence of Molly O'Brien and proceeded to rush along with my reading just so that I could find the other Molly O'Brien. As a result, I ended up reading the entire book very quickly. One of the final chapters recorded folklore and superstitions about butter and milk which I would have been sorry to have missed. Thanks to the two Molly O'Briens, I did not miss them.

9 May—Returning to this valley after a few days in London is full of a sense of less. There is little to read in my immediate out of door world here. There are no signs advertising shops, directions or streets. There is nothing that tells me when to stop or when to go. There are few words and no images to catch and distract attention. There is no language to clutter up my thoughts as I walk. There are plenty of shades of green. In this cold and slowly burgeoning springtime there are plenty of blossoms and leaves to observe. This demands a kind of reading but it is not reading with words and letters. The reading of language as a part of my surrounding environment does not exist. The single sign on the corner of our walk has even disappeared in the last few weeks. It was one of the old cast iron signs and it counted the distance to Clonmel in miles. It had not yet been replaced by an aluminium sign with the distance in kilometres. If it had just fallen down, it would be in the vegetation underneath where it had been on its pole. I looked in the grass below, and it is not there. It has been stolen and is probably on its way to decorate an Irish pub somewhere far from here.

12 May—I heard two men at the market complaining about a shop where the man in charge was not to be trusted. They each claimed that they no longer went to his shop unless they had no choice, but even so, they continued to grumble about his untrustworthiness. It seemed they were trying to one up each other with stories of the shopkeeper's behaviour. The one man said "If you bought a paper off him, sure there'd be a page missing." The other man agreed.

13 May—No one ever parks directly in front of the church. On a Sunday, when Mass is on and there are cars parked right through the village and all the way to the bridge, there is always a gap in front of the church. On weekdays, when people stop to do errands and to run in and out of the post office or the shop, no one parks directly in front of the church. People will use the space where no one parks as a place to back in and turn their car around. I do not know if this Not Parking is some sign of respect or if no one does it because no one else does it. I do not know if this is the norm in front of every church or if it is just this village and this church.

14 May—Mickey the Boxer stopped his car and said good morning. He had a trailer attached on the back of his car. There was nothing in the trailer except a spade. He usually just nods or salutes as he passes. He rarely stops to speak to me. Today he commended me for walking out in all weathers. He said the sunshine today was much nicer for me than the rain and cold of the recent weeks. He said "You're looking well on it." I thanked him and said something else. He then said he was getting very deaf. He said he was seventy-seven. I think he was telling me this because he did not hear or understand what I had said in response to his comments. So I said "Seventy-seven? Well, you're looking well on it." He thanked me and drove off down the road with his trailer.

15 May—Trading In is not the expression used for replacing an old car with a newer car. Older people call this Changing Up.

22 May—BRUSCAR is the word printed or painted on litter bins. I never hear anyone use this word. I have never heard anyone say Pick up that Bruscar, or Put that Bruscar in the Bin. I have never heard this word said out loud. We know what it means because it is on a litter bin and we know what the

bin is for. I assume it means Litter but maybe it means Litter Bin. That is how much I do not know even while I know.

26 May—People are still going off to Turkey to get dental work done. It is called Dental Tourism. Even with the price of travel and paying to stay somewhere, it is cheaper than having the same work done here. I do not think as many people are travelling to get their teeth worked on as there were a few years ago. With the New Austerity, I think people are just letting dental work that needs to be done wait. They are not doing it locally and they are not doing it elsewhere. Usually, on these trips, several members of one family are getting things done and several others go with them to make it into a holiday. They have regular places where they stay and regular dentists whom they visit.

John told me about his trip a few weeks ago. His wife and daughter had major dental work done over six days. He did not have anything done himself. He had a lot of time with his grandchildren. I asked if he enjoyed the Turkish food. He said No, no. He said he would never eat it. He had never even tried it. He said they did cook a good steak and that is what he ate every day.

28 May—The growth of everything has gone mad with this heat. Now, with a bit of rain at night, it is even more rampant. The boreen gets narrower as the cow parsley grows and grows. Driving through it means the car is rubbed and fluffed on both sides. The postman is annoyed by it all. I have to wear long trousers and long-sleeved shirts as I walk up the path toward Johnnie Mackin's. I walk with my hands up and over my head. Some days I feel that I am plunging through water. It is like water because I am surrounded by it and I am moving through it, but it is not at all like water. Some days I pretend I am being marched along at gunpoint. With my arms up and over my head, I do not have a good sense of balance. My feet trip and slip on stones I cannot see. I would not be able to see them even if my arms were not up in the air because the vegetation is so thick. With my arms in the air, I do not find my usual centre. The slipping is wilder and less containable. The slipping feels dangerous. I use my upper arms to shield my face from nettles and brambles. Em is invisible down and underneath the lower level of vegetation. As she gets nearer to me, I see flashes of her black and white colouring just appearing and disappearing in among the dense greenery. When we finally get out and onto the more open path, we are both wet and covered with bits of blossoms, leaves and sticky stems.

29 May—A child, or indeed any person, who is making a lot of noise and calling attention to herself or himself is called a Notice Box. It is not a positive thing to be called a Notice Box. Calling attention to oneself is a way of standing out in the crowd. A lot of traditional socialization here is about blending in and being like everyone else. A Notice Box is not a good thing to be.

2 June—The Lithuanian woman who is doing repairs and clothing alterations is the only one who is busy. She is very good at what she does. Everyone is having clothes shortened or somehow adjusted. People are taking care with what they have as there is little money to buy new things. The clothing shops are devoid of customers. Even with great reductions in price being offered, no one is buying anything. The seamstress told me that she was up until four in the morning trying to catch up with all the work.

4 June—Dirt is not called Dirt. Dirt is called Clay. Soil is another word for dirt, but soil is also called clay. Dirt implies filth. Dirt is synonymous with excrement. It is not polite to say that you have been Digging in the Dirt. Clay is a common natural material which comes from the earth. Clay is used to make things like bricks and pots and plates and other ceramic things. There are lots of degrees of fineness in types of clay throughout the world. Around here, clay is what you dig in order to plant your vegetables.

5 June—The fish shop down on the quay has been owned and run by John Wall for many years. Now it has a new name and a new owner. I knew John Wall would not be lasting much longer when he stopped displaying his fish in his glass-fronted case. Instead, he left it in boxes in the cool store room. The guessing game for customers about which fish he had and how fresh it was became a struggle. No one could see the fish. He knew what he had. He expected his customers to have the same knowledge. If you asked what he had, he would ask what you wanted. It was getting difficult to buy any fish at all from John Wall. The new owners have a sign painted over the window which reads: No Bones. No Skin. No Fear.

22 June—The longest day was a sorry joke. The sky was so dark that even the chickens went to bed earlier than usual.

23 June—The blacksmith has wide double gates in front of his working yard. On the gates he has large letters cut out of steel. They

are beautifully made capital letters: simple, straight and even. The letters are welded onto the top edges of the gates. O.FLYNNS is on one gate and IRON.WORKS is on the other. All the letters are capital letters but the S of O'Flynns and the S at the end of Ironworks are larger capital letters than the other capital letters. After the O there is a full stop which is a tidy small square. It is easier to have made a full stop than an apostrophe and the meaning of the full stop is understood. More confusing is the full stop between IRON and WORKS.

25 June—The English say Mum. Americans say Mom. Here it is Mam, or Mammy. It is also Ma and Da. Once adult, a formality creeps in. I first heard one young man speak of The Mother and The Father when discussing his parents. It sounded nearly biblical. Now I note that this same formality pops up often in conversation. It was not just a characteristic of that young man and his one family. It is most odd when heard on an answer phone, for example: The Mother and I are not available at this time.

26 June—Aiden was trying to explain to us how the old house in its dilapidation and neglect had been frightening to them as children. He said it was a scary house. He said again and again that it was a scary house. He could not find the words to explain exactly why it was a scary house. Eventually he summed it up.

He said, "It was the kind of house that was full of Cats and Jam Jars and Vines." He said, "The Whole Entire Place was frightening."

30 June—A visiting dog always takes over the sheep's wool bed, which we call The New Bed. It is not a New Bed any longer but it is newer than the old bed, so the name New Bed continues. I have never seen a visiting dog crawl into the other bed, which is a wicker basket with scruffy blankets in it. I have never seen a visiting dog express any interest at all in the old bed. Large dogs and small dogs, every single dog who has visited has settled itself onto the New Bed and gone straight to sleep. Em has never challenged a dog sleeping on this bed. She lets it happen but she does not appear pleased. She wanders around and usually flops down on a rug somewhere nearby. After flopping, she breathes

 heavily and sighs a lot. Eventually the visiting dog will leave, so she knows the New Bed will once again be Her Bed.

1 July—When a new septic tank is being installed, it is traditional to put the blood of a pig into the tank to ensure that it works correctly. If there is not a pig being slaughtered nearby, it is normal to go to a slaughterhouse to fetch a small amount of blood. It is worth the trip to ensure a trouble-free septic system.

2 July—The grass roof has loads of blossoms on it. This damp weather suits the roof growth. The corn flowers are the most beautiful. There are no corn flowers growing anywhere on the ground this year. They are only on the roof. Their bright shade of blue glows against the permanently grey sky.

4 July—Another grey and damp and cool day. I am dreadfully discouraged with this non-summery summer weather. I know many other places are suffering, but I am not feeling generous about other people and their weather problems. I am not interested in the weather of other places. My weather is enough to be thinking about. I walked outside when the postman arrived this morning. I walked outside and I said, "Hello John. What I am doing in this country?" He handed me the post. He pointed out across the valley and said "Look at that colour! That is why you are here."

5 July—There is a fashion for people to make bars in their garden sheds. Some people build a shed just for the purpose of it being a bar. This has been happening for quite a long time. I do not think it is a new fashion but maybe the newer bars are just more plentiful. They are perhaps more glamorous too.

A homemade bar is called a shebeen. We were told of one recently where the woman did not like to go to the pub and the man did not like to drink in the house. They built a shebeen in the yard using 144 old pallets. The man figured out a way to take the pallets apart with a minimum of trouble. On the inside of the shebeen he installed narrow shelves. They lined the shelves with single rows of bottles and cans. They put in an old wood stove for warmth. They used candles and lanterns for light. Neighbours came by in the evening for a few drinks if they saw the lights were on inside. People dropped by on their tractors. Everyone liked it because they could smoke without going outside, which they can no longer do in a regular bar. They also liked it because it was a cheaper way to drink.

It was a popular spot for about a year until it burned down. A new shebeen was built to replace it but now its roof has fallen in. The man has very bad arthritis, so he cannot drink any more. Any incentive to repair the shebeen is gone. I do not know if another one has started up to replace what that neighbourhood has lost.

8 July—For years, we always spoke of the road which sweeps along beside the river into Clonmel as the River Road. We knew exactly which road we were speaking about when we spoke of the River Road. It took us a very long time to notice that no one else called the River Road the River Road. People understood what we were saying and they knew which road we were describing, so no one corrected us, but no one else calls it the River Road. It is the Wood Road. The road has the River Suir running beside it on the left- hand side all the way into town. The road has woods rising uphill beside it on the right-hand side most of the way into town. It could as easily be called the River Road instead of the Wood Road, but it is the Wood Road and not the River Road. We have had to adapt.

11 July—We were down in Cork today. I saw a man with a shopping trolley on wheels. His trolley had been full of sand which he had emptied out onto a red rug. He shaped the sand into the form of a dog lying on its side. His sand dog was about the size of a Labrador. It was not a small dog. He scraped away the excess sand which was not part of the dog. It was all very tidy. He made a little raised area of sand in front of the sleeping sand dog and used small letter forms to spell out the name Sandy.

13 July—A woman I met today told me that she has run out of the jobs for rainy days. She said on these bleak days it is often good to clean out the hot press or do some ironing or finish some kind of job which you have put on the Long Finger.

The Long Finger is the expression used for any number of things that get put off. Putting something on the Long Finger means you might do it tomorrow or you might do it next week or you might leave it on the Long Finger for so long that you never do it at all.

She said there are usually so many of those jobs that you know there is no hope of ever finishing them. But now she has finished all those jobs and the low pressure and grey skies just do not inspire her to think about any other jobs that might need to be done. I know exactly how she feels.

16 July—Em and I walked up through the overgrown and very wet boreen today. I had to wear waterproof trousers even though it was not raining. Everything is so wet. The sky is grey and heavy and it carried the promise of more rain. We struggled all the way up. There was no part of the walking which was not a struggle. I took my secateurs and did some clipping on the way but the next time I go up there, I must carry a saw. There is a lot to do to clear the path for upright walking. When we came out of the undergrowth and on to the clear track, I saw that Em's back was covered with slugs. There were big slugs and small slugs. They were all grey. They were riding along on her wet back just because they had been knocked off the wet vegetation. I wiped them off. I do not know if I was carrying slug passengers on my back and on my head too. I did not even think of that until now.

20 July—On these summer nights the sky is still bright at ten or ten thirty at night. When someone goes to bed before the very late darkness falls, it is said that They are Going to Bed in the Brightness.

21 July—I was told about a man named Handmade Condon. He was famous in the area for making fine shoes. When I mentioned him to two people here, they started to argue about him. One of them was convinced that he made clothes and the other was certain that he made shoes. I was mostly interested in him for his name.

22 July—Em is in terrific health again. She seems to be getting younger and younger. After months of worrying that I was living with an elderly, slow and deaf dog, she is in better shape than ever. She has learned to live with her deafness. I no longer believe it is complete deafness. When we walk she turns her head to look over her shoulder to keep track of where I am. Sometimes she looks over her right shoulder and sometimes she looks over her left shoulder. I do the exact same thing if I am the one in the front. We keep an eye on each other.

Some remarks on *Living Locally*

"*Living Locally* offers a new perspective on the art of living that lives with the making of your art, which has always intrigued me."
—Kyle Schlesinger, Cuneiform Press

"In its wry insistence, page after page, on the comic inadequacy of human attempts to classify phenomena, *Living Locally* disavows narrative authority in favour of a fluent responsiveness to local life. The book shines a light on the brimming epiphanic potential of seemingly banal encounters and daily observations. By identifying the repetitions of her own creative practice with these other human and nonhuman patterns of behaviour, Erica Van Horn undermines the privileged perspective conventionally granted to artist and local alike, while remaining puckishly alert to the charms, ironies and hypocrisies involved in the ongoing negotiations of place and habit that add up to living locally."
—Julie Bates, Trinity College Dublin

"Erica Van Horn… became immersed in the slower rhythms of Irish rural life, and has captured something essential and elemental in this funny, colourful, gentle book, simply and quietly told, an ethnography of the Irish soul."
—Neil Sentance, *Caught by the River*

"…Van Horn is, to use the local parlance, a blow-in and her entries are tinged with that sense of unpeeling a new country, while also clearly belonging there and knowing its rhythms. In a way, it captures my favourite thing about being an immigrant—the feeling that you're on both sides of the glass, looking in from the outside, but seeing your reflection as if you were at once in both scenes. As well, it captures that peculiar quirkiness that is rural anywhere, but particularly rural Ireland."
—Jane Flanagan, *Ill Seen, Ill Said* blog

"A very special work from a visual writer whose relationship to her surroundings: land, road, place, sky, dog, neighbours is as rich as her interior life. A heart/eye connection on the page."
—Sarah Schulman, writer and activist